Prokofiev

S. Prokofiev. The last photograph. Taken at Nikolina Gora in the autumn of 1952

Prokofiev

CLAUDE SAMUEL

Translated by Miriam John

Illustrated Calderbook CB 74

CALDER AND BOYARS · LONDON

First published in Great Britain in 1971
by Calder & Boyars Ltd
18 Brewer Street, London W1

Originally published in French in 1960
by Editions du Seuil Paris

© Editions du Seuil 1960
© This translation Calder & Boyars Ltd 1971

ISBN 0 7145 0489 0 Cloth edition
ISBN 0 7145 0490 4 Paper edition

Printed in Great Britain by
Fletcher and Son Ltd, Norwich

Prokofiev

CLAUDE SAMUEL

Contents

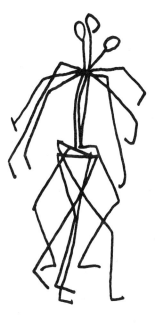

A PASSPORT

Extract from Larionov's sketch-book for the ballet 'Chout'

Ignorance of an important part of the work of Prokofiev persists as one of the many consequences of the 'cold war'. Woe to the artist who is mixed up in the game of politics! According to the date and circumstances of their composition, his works will be those of a genius or of a decadent and his every gesture will be interpreted as the unmistakeable sign of commitment to some doctrine or another.

This is the fate at present reserved for the author of *Peter and the Wolf*. It was tempting, of course, for ill-intentioned spirits to choose as their target an artist who had lived and composed in turn under the Tsarist régime, in the United States of America, in Eastern Europe and in the Soviet Union. But Prokofiev himself outwitted these dark designs by distributing his masterpieces very evenly. His *Scythian Suite* he bequeathed to the Holy Russian Empire, but France and Germany inspired *The Flaming Angel* and Soviet Russia *Alexander Nevsky* and the *Piano Sonata No. 9*. It might seem surprising that the charming *Contes de la Vieille Grand'mère*, so redolent of the Russian soil, should have been composed among the New York skyscrapers, but it was in his homecountry, torn by revolution, that Prokofiev conceived the scenario for *The Love of Three Oranges*, based on a harshly comic story by the Venetian Carlo Gozzi.

In short, Prokofiev has cocked a snook at theorists; they must bow to the evidence. In spite of the process of evolution which takes place in every artist, his work shows a remarkable aesthetic unity. This unity may have been masked from time to time by political attitudes, but no change of régime has ever eclipsed the great invariable in Prokofiev's work: Russia. Tsarist or Communist—what was the difference? A society's structural changes do not alter its deeper characteristics in a dozen years or so and André Siegfried rightly emphasised not long ago that 'the greatest difficulty seems to me to lie in distinguishing what is properly Communist from what is properly Russian. Behind the Soviet phase is still to be found a permanent national spirit'.

The musician, when it comes to the point, lies down readily with the sociologist. Prokofiev, the Soviet composer and glorifier of the Communist régime, is the direct descendant of the musicians of old Russia, of the Glinkas and Moussorgskys. 'One must have a passport', declared Igor Stravinsky, knowing where it would hurt. Prokofiev had a ready answer to this assault. Haughty and discreet, he was never a party to pseudo-national sentimentality, but his return to Soviet Russia and the political imperatives to which he had to defer are the measure of his attachment to his country. To understand Prokofiev's character and explain the development of his musical aesthetic, one must never lose sight of this essential evidence.

'I find pleasure in looking at an uncultivated field. It represents possibilities'
—Victor Hugo.

Ten Centuries of Tradition

TEN CENTURIES OF TRADITION

In 1839 the Marquis de Custine was travelling through Russia. He glimpsed a few moujiks and met the Tsar, who made the following observation to him: 'You probably believe that submission means uniformity in this country; do not be deceived. There is no country where you will find such diversity of race, custom, religion and temperament as in Russia. Variety resides at the root; uniformity is on the surface and unity is merely an appearance. Over there you see twenty officers: the first two only are Russian; the next three are reconciled Poles; some of the others are Germans; even Khans of Kirghisia bring their sons here to be brought up among my young officers. There is one over there.'

The racial diversity of Nicholas I's troops is not an isolated factor. Russian music, too, before it acquired its very marked characteristics, stemmed from a variety of sources. It was born under the sign of a complex conjunction, not with Glinka as is currently accepted, but with that period during the tenth and eleventh centuries when a prodigious artistic and cultural treasure was being laid up. Two cities, Kiev and Novgorod, emerge at that time from the vast areas taken over by successive invaders—Goths, Huns or Tartars. Kiev particularly has links with Byzantium and Scandinavia, enriched by Bulgar culture (the tenth century is the 'golden age' of Bulgaria) and with the Orient as far as Persia—even as far as India. The road over the Carpathians cuts a way towards Hungary and Italy. This privileged situation is carried over into

Extract from Larionov's sketch-book for the ballet 'Chout'

the domain of literature and music. Kiev has, in the Bylinas, its 'chansons de geste' and the story of Prince Igor is its 'Chanson de Roland'.

After the twelfth century, however, comes decline. Music, rich as it is, is largely liturgical, and the Bishop Cyril Tourovsky is to sign its death warrant when, after a dream which is interpreted as a heavenly sign (a simple but effective stratagem) he decrees that music is an emanation from Hell. Artists had the choice of flight or deportation. If they insisted on remaining in the towns, they became mere objects of ridicule.

Prudently, the musicians took to more hospitable shores and so began an enormous movement of decentralisation, followed by the constitution of the very 'people's heritage' which was to re-emerge six centuries later. Moreover, the close relations which had long existed between peasants and masters had already favoured the escape of artistic means of expression to the people.

Spontaneity and exuberance, so characteristic of the Russian temperament, ensure that masterpieces of unknown origin retain their liveliness. When the Glinkas, Moussorgskys and Prokofievs encounter them again, they have lost none of their vitality. On the contrary: six centuries of sleep have preserved their purity and youthfulness.

Whilst the true musical tradition was showing itself in village fêtes and workaday songs, Western art penetrated hesitantly into aristocratic circles. Tsar Michael, the first of the Romanovs, lured a few French and German singers to his Court and received the first harpsichord players; but with a brutal reversal of policy his son, Tsar Alexis, following in the steps of Bishop Cyril Tourovsky, called for the total destruction of all musical instruments.

'If there be any domras, sournas, flutes, guslis or *gueules* in a house, their owner shall publicly burn them or be condemned to the bastinado. . . . Whoever shall permit himself to play one of these instruments shall be excommunicated and anathemised by the Church.'

Punishment by the knout for playing the flute was the sad fate awaiting Russian music-lovers at a time when the West boasted musicians of the order of Schütz, Monteverdi, Marc-Antoine Charpentier. Happily, these prohibitions were soon withdrawn by Tsar Alexis himself. After his remarriage he underwent a sudden change of heart and in turn his son, Peter the Great, opened the Russian frontiers to music. The fashion was for open-air concerts given by foreign orchestras; lavish spectacles were organised where music found a natural place. But of Russian music there was no question: held in very low esteem, it was sedulously ignored. Italian opera followed on French romantic music. Locatelli was received at Saint Petersburg; Martini and Cimarosa held the honours. Finally, it was to an Italian, the Venetian Caterino Cavos, that the task fell, not of revealing their own music to the Russians, but of proving to them that a musician can make good use of a Russian subject for an opera. True, his *Cosaque versificateur* is not an immortal masterpiece, but it does herald the *Ivan Sussanin* (*A Life for the Tsar*) of Glinka.[1]

Glinka defined his own rôle with the remark: 'I should like to unite in the legitimate bonds of marriage the Russian popular song with the good old Western fugue. We are at the people's service to arrange such a marriage!'

Glinka rediscovered folklore, the unique source of national inspiration, and introduced into Russian music themes from the people and their history. *A Life for the Tsar* opened a road which was to lead to *Alexander Nevsky* and *War and Peace* by way of *Boris Godounov* and *Prince Igor*.

One can hardly overlook in the work of Glinka and his successors their predilection for operatic spectacle or, more particularly, the importance of opera in their total output. There is a feeling for the theatre there, of course, but also a desire to create living canvases where the Russian people are constantly depicted. When recent decrees imposed severe restrictions on the work of Soviet musicians, these simply brought about a return, in a sense, to the tradition of Glinka, Borodin or Moussorgsky. The author of *Boris* was already writing: 'It is the Russian people I want to portray. When I am sleeping, I see them in my dreams; when I am eating, I think of them; when I am drinking(!) it is they who appear to me in all their reality, tall, big, majestic, magnificent, without paint or show.'

After having lived in willing ignorance of their folklore, Russian musicians were now to seize avidly upon it and, with equal zeal, cry with Tchaikovsky: 'I am Russian, Russian to the marrow of my bones!' How can one pin the badge of nationalism on a composer studying orchestration with Berlioz and Wagner, construction with Beethoven and philosophy with Schumann? However, paradoxically again, the Russians themselves consider that the author of *Eugene Onegin* truly incarnates the art of their country. This would be enough to demonstrate how every Russian musician achieves a balance between strictly national elements, made up in general of borrowings from folklore and the choice of subject, and an aesthetic derived from the great Masters of the West. Each and every Russian musician treads Glinka's path again in his own way.

The birth of national sentiment in Russia is first and foremost the result of a historical situation. Both Glinka and Pushkin, promoters of a fresh burgeoning of music and literature, were adolescents in the very act of growing (that is, they were particularly receptive) when Napoleon was driven from their country. Militarily and diplomatically, Russia was becoming the equal of Prussia or England; it was logical that its culture should seek a new vigour within itself.

The nineteenth century, when the spread of ideas was so intense in Moscow and Saint Petersburg, saw wave upon wave of musicians and writers with widely differing temperaments and ideas.

[1]Caterino Cavos himself wrote an *Ivan Sussanin* (1815).

School of Novgorod, 14th century

The national and revolutionary stream of autodidactic musicians adhering to the group known as The Five was followed by a series of musicians owing more to foreign aesthetic standards, albeit of unequal value, of whom the most celebrated representatives were Tchaikovsky, Scriabin, Liadov and Glazounov. Most of these played an important part in Prokofiev's development. Some of them were his actual teachers, but all of them were sacred figures when the young Sergei began his course at the Conservatoire. Scriabin in particular personified a taste for hypersensibility and exaltation which earned him passionate devotees.

To this musical movement there attached itself the poetic symbolism of Balmont, who inspired some of Prokofiev's songs, and of Valerie Brioussov, whose ideas were barred by Diaghilev from *Le Monde Artiste*. Here was a profound reaction against the national aspirations of the earlier trend; in fact, *Le Monde Artiste*: 'professed the cult of the individual which constituted the alpha and omega of the new generation', and Diaghilev declared:

'Anyone who wants to understand us must cease to claim that, like Narcissus, we love only ourselves. We love everything . . . but we perceive everything through ourselves. Only in this sense do we love ourselves.'

The measure of the gulf separating these musicians from the members of The Five is the fact that they nearly all, with the exception of Tchaikovsky, neglected the lyrical form of expression and in fact Scriabin, for example, abandoned it altogether. But it is understandable that the following generation, by a healthy reaction, rediscovered an aesthetic nearer to that of Moussorgsky or Rimsky-Korsakov. In the years around 1910 poetry experienced a similar movement, claiming, through the work of Mikhail Alexeivitch Kuzanin, 'a return to the serene clarity of Pushkinian verse'.

Born under the sign of anti-romantic and anti-impressionist reaction, the composers of this new wave nevertheless took divergent paths. To the multiform but profoundly innovating genius of Stravinsky was opposed the Soviet academism of Shostakovitch, whereas Sergei Prokofiev, accused now of revolutionary tendencies, now of neo-classicist leanings, was able to merge traditional forms, romantic accents and contemporary idiom in an absolutely personal style.

A Child of Holy Russia

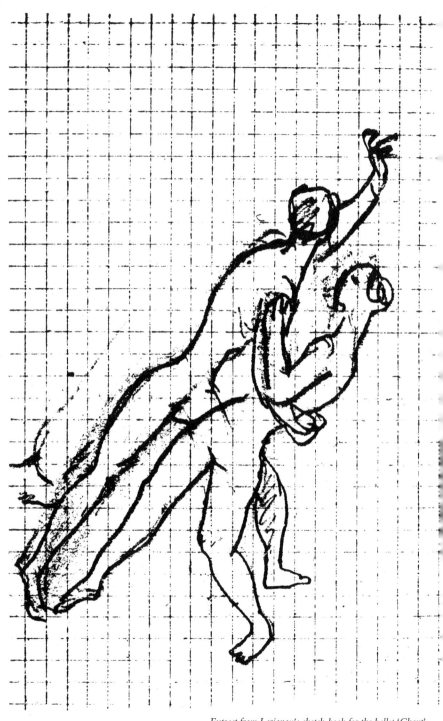

Extract from Larionov's sketch-book for the ballet 'Chout'

A CHILD OF HOLY RUSSIA

Sergei Prokofiev was born in 1891 (the year of the centenary of Mozart's death) in Sonsovka, a small village situated in the basin of the Donetz. Any hidden significance in these dates must surely have to do with the stamp of musical precocity.

In this same year, Russian music was in favour, thanks to one of its most illustrious representatives, Peter Ilyitch Tchaikovsky, who inaugurated Carnegie Hall, New York, on the 5th May. The author of the *Classical Symphony* and of *Romeo and Juliet* thus enjoyed a dual privilege.

A man of precision, Prokofiev has noted in his memoires that he first saw the light of day on Wednesday, 23rd April, at five in the afternoon. His father was originally from Moscow. After studying at the renowned School of Agriculture of Petrovsk-Razoumovsky, he had secured a post as agricultural engineer in the important region of Sonsovka. He was a withdrawn man, stern-looking and silent, whose whole life was devoted to science.

Maria Grigorievna Prokofiev, the mother of the composer, is described by Gliere, Prokofiev's first teacher, as 'a tall woman with magnificent, intelligent eyes . . . who knew how to create around herself a warm, natural atmosphere'.[1] After losing her first two daughters, she had decided to devote her life to music and, each year, she would spend

[1] The reminiscences of Gliere in *Sergei Prokofiev. Autobiography. Articles. Reminiscences.*

Prokofiev's parents in the garden at Sonsovka

two months in Moscow or Saint Petersburg to take piano lessons. She was, apparently, a good performer and would play over every evening her favourite pieces, the sonatas of Beethoven or the waltzes of Chopin, to soothe the young Sergei to sleep. Sometimes, as she was practising, her son would run up to her crying: 'I like that little piece, we'll say it's mine.' Or she would find Sergei installed next to the piano eagerly awaiting the moment when he could take over from his mother and let his imagination run riot.

'One day', Madame Prokofiev writes, 'when I had finished playing, he came up to me, held out a piece of paper and said, "Here's a Chopin mazurka I've composed. Play it to me!" I put the piece of paper in front of me and began to play one of the Chopin mazurkas. "No, not that! Play the Chopin mazurka I've written!" I replied that I couldn't play what he had written because that was not how one composed, but I saw he was near tears, and had to show him the mistakes he had made in his notation. "Look, you've written ten lines without separating the bars. You must write five lines for each hand and each bar must be separate".[1]

We can already see the creative instinct emerging in the child; he had a marvellous memory and limitless imagination. With the help of a few short theory lessons from Madame Prokofiev, he was writing his first composition when he was six—an *Indian Gallop* in F Major from which only the B flat is missing, because his small fingers could not reach the black notes on the piano (unless he was already feeling the necessity to extend the traditional tone-range). But his mother, like a good musician, hastened to correct the mistake. The *Indian Gallop* was inspired by a famine which was ravaging India. Conversation and the papers everywhere were full of it.

In the summer of the same year, a friend of the Prokofievs came to spend a few weeks at Sonsovka and Madame Prokofiev was to recall later the precocious creative will of the composer at that time: 'We would often play duets together', she writes, 'and Sergei used to love listening to us. He would often leave the toys we had put out for him and come and stand near us, listening and looking with wide-open eyes. One day, fascinated by our playing, he said to me: "I want to compose a march for four hands." I explained to him that it was more difficult to write for four hands than for two. "I'll write it just the same!" A few days later, he presented us with a *March in C Major for Four Hands* ending in a long *glissando* stretching over two octaves.'[1]

As good luck would have it, Sergei had a remarkable teacher in his mother. She knew how to dispense with boring exercises and, in accordance with good pedagogic principles, imposed on her son no more than twenty minutes' practice a day. Even so, Sergei's progress was considerable. He read music easily and was soon playing a few pages of Mozart, then the easier sonatas of Beethoven. More than anything he loved to improvise in front of his parents' friends, but they had to listen, or he would stop abruptly and leave the piano for good—a small flash of temperament from the great artist to come, who was always to retain a somewhat pernickety disposition.

The child's gifts aroused the admiration of all of 'musical Sonovska' and yet, in spite of the value of his mother's teaching, Prokofiev declared later on that *nothing was done thoroughly* and that the position of his hands at the piano was very bad. Hardly surprising!

In 1899, when Sergei was eight years old, his parents went to Moscow and decided to take him with them. After a long journey came the dazzling sight! Which were most to be admired—the fabulous monuments or the countless churches? Truth to tell, Prokofiev, who was never passionately interested in the art treasures of the great capitals, was already thinking exclusively of music and the only shock he experienced

[1]The reminiscences of Madame Prokofiev (idem).

was in the Grand Opera House. There, he discovered in quick succession *The Sleeping Beauty*, *Prince Igor* and *Faust*, the duel scene from which made a profound impression on him.

No sooner was he back in Sonsovka than Sergei affirmed: 'I want to write my opera!'

'How can you write an opera?', asked his mother, 'why do you have such impossible ideas?'

'You'll see, you'll see!'

Without more delay, he produced a libretto 'in verse', written out in a childish script; he then composed the music and, three or four months later, presented his parents with *The Giant*, an opera in three Acts and six Tableaux for solo piano. The subject, according to Madame Prokofiev, reveals the child's fertile imagination.

Madame Prokofiev records an incident connected with the writing of the libretto. At the end of his story, Sergei had invented the defeat of an all-powerful King by the redoubtable Giant. Now, 'at that time of extremely strict monarchy', writes Madame Prokofiev, 'this idea was not approved by the paternal authority and the young composer, very much put out by this censorship, would not consent to write an ending involving a reconciliation between the Giant and the King.'

The dearest wish of any author-composer must surely be to attend a performance of his work. Fortune smiled on Sergei Prokofiev. The following summer, he 'conducted' at his uncle's house, during the holidays, the 'première' of *The Giant*. The good man, somewhat amazed and filled with admiration, commented: 'When your operas are performed on the Imperial stage, don't forget you made your début at my place!'

The success enjoyed by *The Giant* encouraged the boy to continue along the road to opera; inspired by a subject rich in sensational incidents, storm and shipwreck, he composed *On the Desert Islands*.

However, these attempts were still nothing but childish games. Sergei was growing up and his parents, confident of his vocation, decided to give him a formal musical education. They took him to Moscow, to a pupil of Taneyev, a man named Pomerantsev, whose mission it was to present their son to his teacher. Taneyev, a composer of talent and future director of the Bolshoi Theatre in Moscow, was an important personage in Moscow society. He agreed to meet the Prokofievs and to hear the *Overture to the Desert Islands*. Sergei, in no way intimidated by the presence of his illustrious colleague, recognised that Taneyev, who had artfully crammed him with chocolate, was *kind, slightly mocking, but not in the least frightening;* then, after the audition, the Master recommended to Madame Prokofiev that she should cultivate her son's abilities. He advised her to engage Pomerantsev as his teacher. For three years, Taneyev followed the boy's compositions with interest. From time to time, Sergei made his way to Moscow, with his mother, in order to visit him.

'Show me what you have written for us, my little Sergei.'

And Sergei, quite unruffled, would bring out his music and show it.

'Very good', Taneyev would say, 'now let's play.'

Side by side, the massive Taneyev and the small, pale boy, take their places at the piano; they play, discuss and, finally, Taneyev asks:

'What are you going to write next?'

'A military march. I know a Lieutenant who's promised to play it with his band.'

'A military march? I've never written one of those; how will you do it?'

'I've already found out all about the instruments and—I'm going to compose it!'

Aged nine, with the score of 'The Giant'

'I'll help you. I've got a score for a military march. You're going to take it away with you to the country and give it back to me next year.'

The first lessons with Pomerantsev were received coldly, for the child was by no means seduced by the charms of harmony. 'I wanted to compose operas with marches, storms, complicated scenes, and here I was tied hand and foot with tedious rules.'[1]

Pomerantsev was swiftly replaced by a young student teacher who came straight from Moscow at the invitation of the Prokofievs. He was the composer Reinhold Glière. Prokofiev always remembered with affection the lessons he had with the young master. Forty years later he wrote: 'All Glière's students remember his teaching with pleasure because, like a true pedagogue, he knew how to enter into the mind of his pupil. He did not inflict on him any dry theories which he could and should know for himself, so long as he was not receptive to them. Glière could guess where the interests of his pupils lay and strove to develop them in the right direction.'[1]

He would also intersperse the lessons with chess and croquet matches and finally won Sergei's heart by accepting a challenge to a duel with pistols. But he was above all a far-sighted pedagogue, combining theoretical instruction with free composition and allowing the young boy to pursue the development of his personality.

Glière arrived in Sonsovka at the beginning of the summer of 1902. In his reminiscences, he describes his first contact with the Prokofiev family:

'I got off the train at the little station of Grichino, not far from the town of Bachmont, with my humble baggage, comprising a huge bundle of manuscript paper and a violin. A two-horse carriage had been sent for me from Sonsovka. The road lay between the magnificent fields and meadows of the "Black Country", all scattered with flowers. All the way along the road, for a distance of twenty-five kilometres, I never ceased to admire the marvellous spectacle of the Ukrainian landscape, so rich in colour. At last there appeared on a hill a small manorial hall surrounded with the cheerful greenery of a garden and flanked by out-houses and a large open shed. From the very first moment, I felt at home.'

According to Glière's reports, life in the Prokofiev household was 'strict, but intelligent'. One got up early and went for a bathe in the river before breakfast. From ten o'clock until eleven, Sergei worked with his music teacher before taking Russian and arithmetic with his father. His mother then took him for his French and German lessons. The afternoon was devoted to recreation: horseback rides, chess games or long turns on stilts, for which Sergei showed a particular preference. Every Sunday, a carriage was prepared and the whole family visited the neighbouring properties of Sonsovka.

[1]*Sergei Prokofiev. Autobiography* (idem).

These long trips across country often led the young musician among peasants singing lovely Ukrainian melodies, and 'these first childhood impressions cut deep into the mind of a child so sensitive to beauty. There is no doubt that they contributed to his artistic development and to the awakening of his creative consciousness. No less certain is it that these musical impressions from his childhood gave the future composer his sharp and profound sense of the language of popular music.'

During his three months' stay at Sonsovka, Gliere taught Sergei musical construction and orchestration, tidied up his harmonies, which were somewhat confused, and finally gave him some judicious advice in the composition of various small pieces, such as the *Little Songs* in which Nestiev already discerned, alongside the 'combined influences of Schubert, Schumann, Bellini and Verdi, an unquestionable personality'.

So piano lessons played an important part in these first studies. But Gliere was not a pianist. He had noticed the bad technique of his pupil without being able really to remedy it. All the lessons were unfortunately broken off at the end of the summer, and Gliere returned to Moscow, leaving instructions with Madame Prokofiev. However, he remained in constant touch with the young musician and four letters from Sergei make it possible to follow the child's work and development during the winter of 1902-03. At times, Sergei's correspondence leads us to subjects outside music. On 29th March, he wrote to Gliere:

Dear Reinhold Mauricevitch,
I send you all my greetings for the coming Easter and hope you will be spending it pleasantly. Thank you for the stamps you sent me. There are so many that I haven't been able to count them or sort them yet. But I've found several foreign stamps I didn't have before, for instance, the Mexican ones and the ones from India, Canada, New Zealand, Ceylon and a lot of other countries. Please allow me to offer you a free seat in the first row at all my public performances.

For Mama's return I have finished my Violin Sonata; although the first part is in C minor, I have written the finale in the major key because I don't seem able to write a presto in the minor. Tchaikovsky's second Symphony also begins in C minor and ends in C major. I have also written a second little song for the second series. I like music dictation very much and, for the moment, am doing very well. Papa, Mama and Mademoiselle send their greetings.

I shall not be doing any school work during April and shall do some more composing, as you said I should.
Your loving
Sergei[1]

In June 1903 Gliere came back to Sonsovka. The lessons, the tours of the countryside and the games began again. During the preceding winter,

[1]The reminiscences of Gliere (idem).

Sergei had composed a *Sonata for Piano and Violin* which master and pupil performed before a public consisting entirely of the Prokofiev family. The work enjoyed a decided success and the composer had to 'come back several times to acknowledge applause'. According to Gliere, one of the themes of this Sonata was to be taken up again later in the *Ballad for Violin Op.* 15.

But this summer of 1903 is remarkable for the composition of two important works: a true *Symphony* in four movements and an opera *The Orgy during the Plague*, after Pushkin. Taneyev, commenting on the *Symphony*, imprudently reproached Prokofiev for his over-simple harmonies. Prokofiev was never to forget the remark. He deepened his researches into harmony and, eight years later, the same Taneyev was affirming, with a hint at his own culpability, that the *Studies, Op.* 2 are 'crammed with false notes'. *The Orgy during the Plague*, finished in the following year, was a more ambitious work, although in only one Act, of which the Overture occupies the greater part; but its author derived a certain feeling of pride from it and accepted its comparison with the opera which the same subject inspired in Caesar Cui, whose score he followed with 'avidity, jealousy and a critical mind. The song of Mary', he remarks, 'having the same mood, the same subject and the same melodic line, resembles mine. He did not bring off that passage very well, I told my mother.'[1]

Sergei was twelve years old; his studies must now continue in a Conservatoire. Two establishments offered themselves for the Prokofievs' choice: the first, in Moscow, was headed by Taneyev, whilst the second, at Saint Petersburg, was under the direction of Rimsky-Korsakov. For a while, nothing was decided except that the boy should pass the winter in Moscow to prepare his entrance examination. Then, at the beginning of the year 1904, Madame Prokofiev took her son to Saint Petersburg to see Glazounov and, upon his advice, she decided, in agreement with Taneyev, to enter him at the Conservatoire in that city. But the choice of Saint Petersburg had not been dictated solely by academic considerations; in fact, Madame Prokofiev, who did not wish to be parted from her son, planned to stay with her sister Tatiana Gregorievna in Saint Petersburg. A little later on, however, Sergei and his mother rented a small flat in the Rue Sadovaia.

The lessons with Gliere were now over. Master and pupil were to remember them for a long time and continued to exchange a few letters each year. But the child of Holy Russia, the darling of Sonsovka, must make his entrance into the 'official' world of music, an entrance which was to burst noisily upon it.

[1] *Sergei Prokofiev. Autobiography* (idem).

I Abhor Imitation

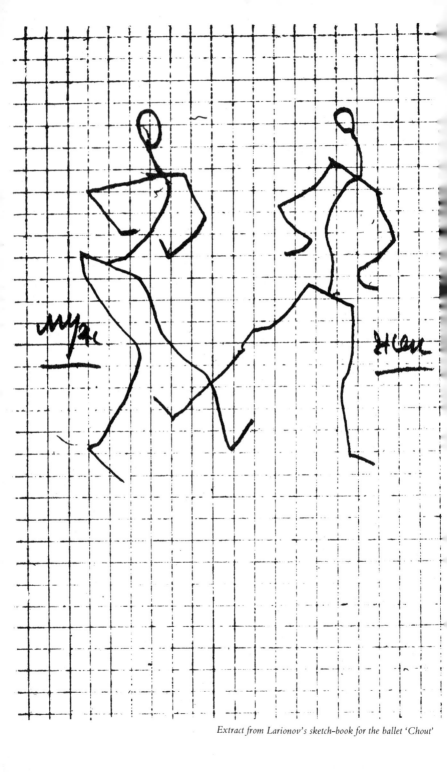

Extract from Larionov's sketch-book for the ballet 'Chout'

I ABHOR IMITATION . . .

In 1869 Antoine Rubinstein received letters-patent saluting 'exceptional services to music'. This distinction was an acknowledgment of his efforts towards the creation of the first musical Conservatoire in Russia rather than of the composition of nineteen operas and six symphonies now fallen into well-earned oblivion. In fact, on his return to Saint Petersburg in 1849 after several trips abroad, Rubinstein had embarked on an active campaign in favour of official education in music. The project was not to come to fruition until thirteen years later, on the founding of the Saint Petersburg Conservatoire. The new establishment became, thanks to the influence of the cosmopolitan Rubinstein, a bastion of Germanic culture in opposition to The Five, but the citadel of Western art did not put up very great resistance to the national spirit which was now enlivening Russian music and soon the Rimsky-Korsakovs, the Glazounovs, the Liadovs, were charged with the responsibility of forming the new generation of composers.

It was into this young school that Sergei found his way during the autumn of 1904. Some months earlier, his parents had introduced him to Glazounov, but the first encounter with the Master had not been particularly cordial. Glazounov had listened attentively to the efforts of the young musician and had then congratulated him somewhat curtly. Some days later, however, he visited Madame Prokofiev and advised her to enrol her son at the Saint Petersburg Conservatoire, adding, as legend has it: 'He will become a great artist!' In any case, to show his

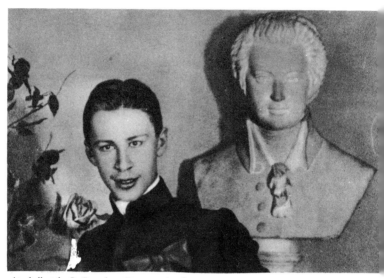

At a ball at the St. Petersberg Conservatoire, January 1908

admiration, he sent Sergei a score of the *Fantasy Waltz* of Glinka, with the dedication: 'To my dear colleague, Sergei Prokofiev, from Glazounov.'

The dear colleague, however, had to pass an entrance examination. Whilst preparing for this, Prokofiev composed a new opera: *Ondine*. The libretto is written in verse, after the *Ondine* of Frédéric de la Motte-Fouqué, by the woman poet Kilchtet, whose acquaintance Sergei had made during his stay in Saint Petersburg. But the score was never finished, owing to a difference of opinion between them.

At last, the examination day arrived. Sergei Prokofiev presented himself, very confident, before a highly intimidating team of adjudicators:

'The entrance examination was conducted in a rather impressive manner. Before myself, they questioned a man with a small beard and a solitary *Romance*, unaccompanied, as his only baggage. I came in, bowed down beneath the weight of two music cases containing four operas, two sonatas, a symphony and a rather large number of piano pieces. "I like this", said Rimsky-Korsakov, who was presiding. They made sure I had a good ear and that I knew how to read the clefs. Then I played my *Ondine* and, as I played, Rimsky-Korsakov, who was seated near me, made a few corrections in pencil. The examination lasted a long time. Rimsky-Korsakov and Glazounov went into an adjoining room several times to talk to my mother. I have an almost stenographic memory of that examination in the form of a letter fifteen pages long which I wrote to my father the same day.'[1]

There is little doubt that a man as orderly as Prokofiev did in fact carefully keep this historic account and that it will one day become the joy of musicologists.

'Every work by Liadov is a precious gem', said Rimsky-Korsakov, not without irony, for this greatly gifted composer was guilty of the sin of sloth. At twenty-three, however, he was a teacher at the Conservatoire of Saint Petersburg and, in this capacity, instructed Prokofiev in harmony and counterpoint. The relation of master to pupil was permanently marred by mutual misunderstanding. After suffering prodigious boredom during a harmony course which the teacher had been conducting without conviction, Sergei finally lost interest. When, years later, he presented Liadov with some compositions bearing the stamp of astonishing originality and audacity, Liadov replied: 'I do not understand why you are studying with me—go and join Strauss and Debussy!' Unimaginable insult! And the tone of the utterance was such, Prokofiev adds, that it really meant 'Go to the Devil!' In short, these harmony lessons were somewhat inharmonious.

Prokofiev consoled himself by cementing a firm friendship with Nikolas Miaskovsky, his elder by ten years, whose advice was more profitable than the 'dry theories of Liadov'. Miaskovsky, the future author of twenty-seven symphonies, was already, on entering the Conservatoire, 'a composer with a little beard and a bulging music-case'. At times irritated by his young colleague, who would draw up accurate statistics of their respective faults, he played a decisive part in Sergei's musical development by revealing to him the work of Richard Strauss, of Claude Debussy and of Max Reger.

Miaskovsky, although a great admirer of Scriabin and the French impressionists, was one of the first to recognise the vigour and health of his friend's work. In 1912, he published in the journal *Music* this comment on *Four Studies for Piano, Opus 2*:

'Here is a work which breathes strength and freshness. With what joy and astonishment one hears this clear, sane work slicing through the sickliness, anaemia and weakness of our time! . . . These magnificent studies demonstrate at one and the same time a strongly marked sense of the fantastic, a tender but gay lyricism, a scourging irony and a powerful attack.'

So Liadov did not appreciate the independent spirit of his pupil. Prokofiev's lessons with other teachers at the Conservatoire, the piano lessons with Winckler and Madame Essipova, the conducting courses with Tcherepnin, the composition with Vitol and Rimsky-Korsakov met with varying fortunes. Rimsky was obviously a 'star' and his teaching so highly valued that it was difficult to follow his explanations. Moreover, Prokofiev was not in the least inclined to do so. He drew no

[1] *Sergei Prokofiev. Autobiography* (idem).

profit from his passage through the class and, in 1908, was hardly able to satisfy the requirements of the examination. Rimsky-Korsakov's note at the time read: 'A gifted student, but lacks maturity.'

Why should Prokofiev bother with Rimsky-Korsakov's classes, since he already considered himself a composer? All his leisure time was devoted to the creation of new work, a *Symphony in E Minor* (no Opus number) and above all the original versions of the *First*, *Third* and *Fourth Piano Sonatas*.

Thanks to Glazounov, the Symphony was performed at a private concert in October 1908 and, if one is to believe the author, the score, 'indifferently instrumented, produced a rather confused impression'. As a matter of fact, Prokofiev was still searching for a style. Being young, he was arrogant and presumptuous, but Miaskovsky tempered his ardours and wisely advised him not to attach too much importance to youthful exercises. 'It is useless', he told him, 'to take the numbering of your sonatas seriously; there will come a time when you will tear them all up and write: Sonata Number One.'

Miaskovsky was right. Prokofiev was soon to open the catalogue of his work and write just that: *Opus One: Sonata Number One for Piano.* He could, in fact, have omitted to number this *Sonata No. 1* in which his personality is so hard to trace. The pianistic writing of the score, dedicated to Morolev, a young veterinary surgeon from Sonsovka, reminds one constantly of Schumann, a Schumann faintly tinged with Liszt, Scriabin and perhaps even Prokofiev. This *Sonata in F minor* consists of one short movement only, the draft of two other movements having been abandoned by the composer. Nevertheless, it is important as opening a series of nine sonatas, an incomparable piano cycle, which, apart from this first movement, is possessed of a notable unity, making nonsense of chronology and of the so-called three periods of Prokofiev's life.

The *Sonata No. 1* was finished in 1909 and was given its first recital by the composer in Moscow on 6th March, 1910. This recital constituted a kind of infidelity to the Saint Petersburg Soirées of Contemporary Music, which in general formed a setting for the propagation of the work of young musicians. At these Saint Petersburg soirées, the issue of the *Monde Artiste* of Diaghilev, it was the modernist Karatyguin who set the tone: contempt for the second generation of The Five and for the bourgeois music of Tchaikovsky; the pursuit, among the classics, of compositions with a striking significance to the minds of the young revolutionaries (such as Moussorgky's *Sunless* cycle) and the discovery of musicians representing 'art nouveau' both in Russia and in the West. Debussy, Schoenberg, Strauss, Stravinsky, Prokofiev, Vincent d'Indy and Scriabin were played indiscriminately.

Prokofiev made his début at these soirées on 31st December, 1908, with the public performance of *Seven Piano Pieces*, *Opus* 3 *and Opus* 4. As a result of this session, the young virtuoso wrote to Gliere:

'. . . On 18th December,[1] at the concert of contemporary music, I played my own work for the first time. You know all the pieces in the programme except for the first and the last, as I played them to you in the autumn. They were successful and the critics treated them kindly.'[2]

In fact, the critics commented: 'The little piano pieces which M. Prokofiev played from his own manuscript are most original. The young composer, who has not finished his artistic studies, belongs to an advanced modernist movement and surpasses in daring and originality the boldest of French contemporaries.' (sic!)

This assessment certainly overwhelmed the young Sergei with joy, for he had always striven to leave the beaten track, having on principle cultivated his originality even when a simple student at the Conservatoire. Later on, he affirms:

'The chief merit of my life (or, if you prefer it, its chief inconvenience) has always been the search for originality in my own musical language. I abhor imitation and I abhor the familiar.'

One might question the authenticity of this originality, that is, whether it created new and fertile forms in the field of contemporary music. In 1908, it is above all noisy and sometimes clumsy, a point picked on with severity by the reviewer of the *Petersburg Journal*: 'Although one has the feeling that these rather disorderly compositions are for polishing the musician's pen, there is to be found in them at times a flash of talent.'

Only the last of the seven pieces executed on 31st December won a wide popularity. It was the *Suggestion diabolique*, a piece of strong pianistic quality, of irresistible dynamism, whose well-defined rhythmicality is already 'pure' Prokofiev.

The composer's comparative daring shocked the Vitols and the Liadovs more and more and the classes at the Conservatoire became totally superfluous. Prokofiev thus left the composition class after having received, at the end of the year 1909, a diploma as 'free artist'. However, at only eighteen, he was not yet capable of enjoying the liberty to which he aspired; once more, he turned to the inevitable Liadov but, after a few free composition courses, discord re-emerged and the rupture was soon complete. The young musician had realised that he would never again learn anything in the way of composition unless on his own. On the other hand, to perfect his piano technique and acquaint himself

---

[1] The difference between 18th and 31st December is merely the thirteen days' difference between the Gregorian and Julian calendars.
[2] The reminiscences of Gliere (idem).

with the principles of conducting an orchestra, he approached two excellent teachers at the Conservatoire: Madame Essipova and Nikolas Tcherepnin.

The fame of Madame Essipova's teaching extended far beyond the narrow limits of the class; she had a perfect knowledge of the piano, a remarkable teaching gift and musical tastes which did not always accord with those of her new pupil. Prokofiev freely allowed her her almost exclusive predilection for Mozart, Chopin and Schubert, but could not forgive her her desire to share it with him:

'The characteristic feature of Madame Essipova's teaching,' he says, 'was to tailor everyone to the same model; true, the model was in good taste.'

Over a period of five years, the lessons of Madame Essipova were rich in diverse incident. The teacher battled at one and the same time against the modernistic tendencies of her pupil and against his disorderly and undisciplined playing. On several occasions, Prokofiev was threatened with expulsion, either because he placed his hands badly, or because he insisted on playing over-audacious work; for example he started a veritable scandal by preparing one of the *Fairy Tales* of Medtner for the class.

The conducting classes took place in a more serene atmosphere. The eclectic tastes of Nikolas Tcherepnin, friend of Glazounov and a fine artist, smoothed out the difficulties, and Prokofiev pondered the wise counsel of his teacher:

'You have no gift for conducting,' confided Tcherepnin, 'but, as I believe in you as a composer, I know that you will sooner or later conduct your own work on more than one occasion; that is why I shall teach you how to do it.'

At the end of his studies, Prokofiev conducted *The Marriage of Figaro* in public, but the reviewers, alas, underwrote the opinion of Tcherepnin.

The author of *Suggestion diabolique* was now the possessor of some solid musical equipment. In the artistic circles of Saint Petersburg, his name was no longer unknown; he appeared a revolutionary because his youth made him intransigent in his ideas. Nevertheless, his musical predilections should not have led him into the perilous paths of 'modernism'. In fact, in 1906, that is, four years after the creation of *Pelléas* and one year after that of Ravel's *Quartet*, when Schoenberg was on the road leading from *Gurre-Lieder* to the *Pierrot Lunaire*, Prokofiev, when questioned by Liadov as to his favourite composers, replied:

Tchaikovsky
Wagner
Grieg

and this reply probably reassured Liadov.

Tchaikovsky
Wagner
Grieg

'I named Tchaikovsky,' explained Prokofiev, 'in all sincerity, although I was far from knowing all his work; I knew only the *Second Symphony* and was quite ignorant of his chamber music.'

'I named Wagner out of snobbery; I had heard that he was interesting and he was much talked of in musical circles, but I had never listened either to the *Ring* or to *Tristan* and I knew little of the *Meistersinger*.'

'I knew the piano work of Grieg quite well.'

Ever since his entry into the Conservatoire, ever since the first Soirées of Contemporary Music, Prokofiev had never ceased to compose: after a *Sinfonietta*, inspired, according to its author, by the

Diaghilev listening to Wanda Landowska in Moscow, 1908 (Detail from a painting by Pasternak)

Sinfonietta of Rimsky-Korsakov ('when I was composing it,' says Prokofiev, 'I wanted to write a nice, easy kind of music'); two pages of symphonic composition: *Dreams* and *Autumnal Sketch*, showing the influence of Scriabin and Rachmaninov; *Two Choruses for female voice Opus 7* and the *Romance Opus 9* based on texts by Balmont[1] whose poetry was a mere 'stream of sounds and play of colours, refreshing but ephemeral' Prokofiev affirms the development of his personality with the *Piano Concerto No. 1.*

Francis Poulenc, who was a friend of the composer, wrote recently: 'In the same way that the First Concerto of Beethoven prefigures his mature work, so the *Concerto No. 1* of Prokofiev classed its author among the ranks of the musical great ones.' But Prokofiev's Concerto is much more than a prefiguration of later work; in spite of a certain awkwardness at times (the grandiloquence of the *Finale,* for example) the orchestration reveals all the characteristics of the author's style: the spring and freshness of the *Allegro brioso* with its magnificent opening theme, the impassioned lyricism of the *Andante,* the assured mastery of the piano writing and the intense, throbbing rhythm.

[1] A second Romance included in *Opus 9* was composed after a text of Apoukhtin

The Concerto was given its first public performance in Moscow on 7th August, 1912, with the composer at the piano; the novelty of the style, and above all the vehement rhythm, took by surprise a public more sensitive to the impressionism of Scriabin than to the pianistic firmness of Prokofiev. Scandal broke loose. The Journal *Music* ardently defended the new composition. Miaskovsky particularly supported 'one of the most original works in the history of piano concerti', whereas Sabaneiev, in *The Voice of Moscow*, declared: 'In my opinion it would be a dishonour to music to give the name to Monsieur Prokofiev's work, which is hard, energetic, rhythmic and coarse.'

Prokofiev's pianistic gift is less disputed than his talents as a composer; his power and authority, his percussive resonance, make a great impression. Again, his playing is particularly suited to his writing for the piano which is reaffirmed in rapid succession by two significant scores: the *Toccata Opus 11* and the *Sonata No. 2 Opus 14*.

The Toccata, extremely difficult to perform, expresses an implacable rhythm by the hammering out of heavy chords:

Sometimes, by way of respite, a light, delicate phrase breaks the powerful rhythm, gently interpolating a patch of freshness.

The *Sonata No. 2 in D Minor Opus 14*, written in the same year, is of vastly superior interest. Despite one or two over-simple formulae and certain awkward phrases, the work abounds in originality, particularly in the pulsating *Vivace*, whose joyous theme is treated with absolute mastery. Two other elements come into play: a tender lyricism in the first and third movements (is not Prokofiev after all a lyric composer?) and the fleeting reference to a folk motif, skilfully introduced.

During the whole of this period, Prokofiev concentrated his attention on the piano. He resumed his previous innovations in the *Ten Pieces, Opus* 12 and the first *Sarcasms*, giving full measure in his *Piano Concerto No. 2*.

When Prokofiev first performed the *Concerto No. 2* at Pavlovsk on 5th September, 1913, under the direction of Aslanov, he unleashed a battle which no doubt reminded him, not without pleasure, of the recent scandal in Paris over the *Sacre du Printemps*. A journalist faithfully reports the scene:

> 'A young man advanced on to the rostrum—he could have been, say, a pupil at the Peterschule. It was Prokofiev. Little by little doubts begin to flit across the mind of the astonished public: some express their indignation out loud, some get up and find salvation in retreat. "This music is one enough to drive one mad!" says someone. Seats are emptied one by one. At last, the Concerto comes to an end on a rumbling chord of wind instruments and amidst an indescribable hubbub. Most of the audience are whistling and shouting angrily.'[1]

All the influential critics are unanimous in condemning without appeal this 'futuristic music'. Like the *Sacre*, the work is performed again fifteen months later—and understood. Assafiev, faithful champion of Prokofiev, writes in *Music*: 'The daring and assurance of the young barbarian captivated and convinced the public, backed up as they were by a spontaneous talent and a fiery performance.' Assafiev does, however, make serious reservations concerning the mediocrity of the instrumentation. We can have no means of contradicting him, since this original version of the *Concerto No. 2* was lost, probably when Prokofiev left Russia; we know only the second version, finished in 1923, and first performed by the

[1]Quoted by Nestiev in *Prokofiev*.

author in Paris on 8th May, 1924, under the direction of Sergei Koussevitsky.

It is very likely that, owing to the strides made by the composer by that time, the instrumentation of the '1923 version' of the Concerto had benefited by improvements. At least, as it now stands, it has none of the orchestral wealth and complexity of the *Buffoon* (*Chout*) or of the *Scythian Suite*. The relative simplicity of the instrumental scoring is a better foil for the solo part, which here achieves an admirable lyricism and depth, nobility of expression and force. Here are the indisputable signs of a talent in full control of its medium. The influence, discreetly suggested, of Liszt and Schumann, is perfectly assimilated into the style of Prokofiev, transfigured since the very Schumannesque quality of the *Sonata No. 1*.

The Concerto comprises four movements: an *Andantino-Allegretto* remarkable for its simplicity and the radiant beauty of the first theme, set against a muted string accompaniment, and especially so for its longdrawn-out cadenza, which presents extraordinary hazards in performance; a smiling, lively *Scherzo*; an *Intermezzo* with characteristic marching rhythms; and finally an *Allegro tempestuoso* in which uninhibited, brilliant movement alternates with lyrical pauses.

After this triumphant achievement, and as a consequence of the Pavlovsk outcry, Prokofiev the pianist left his piano for a time, to compose *Magdalen*, an opera in one act; and the 'Cello Ballad, Opus 15. *Magdalen*, inspired by the Princess Lieven's indifferent novel, has never been published or performed; the orchestration, moreover, is unfinished and the manuscript, written in pencil, is in the hands of Prokofiev's French publisher. The 'Cello Ballad, hardly known any more, was written at the request of the amateur 'cellist Rouzky. It takes the form of a Concerto and was much appreciated by Miaskovsky.

Prokofiev's creative activity is uninterrupted during these last years of study, but at the same time he has to put up with the suspicion of 'thinking' musicians in Saint Petersburg (he was the first to dare to perform Schoenberg during the Soirées of Contemporary Music) and the mistrust of publishers. The six members of the Reading Committee of the house of Koussevitsky, encouraged by Rachmaninov and Medtner, refused to publish his first two works. These met a happier fate with Jurgensson, thanks to the insistence of Taneyev and Gliere; in fact, although he rejected the *Ballad*, Jurgensson purchased the first four works for one hundred roubles; the *Sonata No. 2* for two hundred roubles and the *Five Pieces* of *Opus 12* for five hundred roubles.

So Prokofiev was performed (and booed); published (and paid). What further acknowledgment could his ardent, ambitious nature hope for? An award to salute his pianistic gifts would by no means have displeased him and the prospect of a fresh struggle filled him with delight. When, in fact, he decided to put himself to the redoubtable test of the Rubinstein

Competition in the Spring of 1914, he was aiming at only one place—the first. It could have been in order to achieve this that he began by an unprecedented surprise stroke.

Candidates at the Rubinstein Competition usually prepared a piece from the *Well-Tempered Klavier*, and a classical Concerto. Prokofiev, against all expectation, advised the examiners that he would render a little-known Bach Fugue and his own *Concerto No. 1*. Consternation! Regulations were invoked, but in vain, and the members of the jury, obliged to accept the situation, nevertheless insisted on receiving the score a week before the examination date. Thanks to the speedy operations of Jurgensson, each member was promptly in possession of a copy of the work: Prokofiev was able to embark on the venture. He could now brave the retrograde jury, and if the prize were not awarded to him he could lay the blame at leisure on the obscurantism of the jurors.

On the day of the competition, when Prokofiev appeared on the stage, very sure of himself, he saw twenty scores spread simultaneously on twenty pairs of knees. His dazzling performance plunged the jury into a cruel state of conflict. After a long deliberation in which two opposing forces, each determined not to give way, found themselves confronting one another, the young revolutionary was granted the highest award. Glazounov, furious, refused to make the public announcement of the awards. In the end, after being prevailed upon the change his mind, he came forward on to the rostrum and 'announced the results', according to Prokofiev, 'in a vague and incomprehensible manner'. Some months later, the Concerto was performed under the direction of Tcherepnin during the course of a Soirée devoted to Conservatoire prize-winners.

The young composer, now twenty-three years old, could feel well pleased with himself. In command of a repertoire which already comprised seventeen works, he was now looked upon as the leader of avant-garde music and, with the blessing of the Rubinstein Competition, he had now to take off for the conquest of distant Europe.

A Revolution in Chaldean Terms

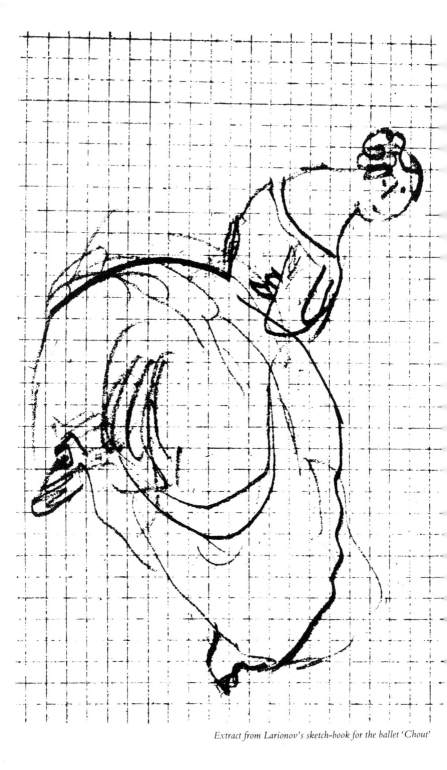

Extract from Larionov's sketch-book for the ballet 'Chout'

A REVOLUTION IN CHALDEAN TERMS

'Astonish me!', cried Diaghilev to Jean Cocteau in 1911, and Diaghilev himself never ceased to astonish people, right up to the sad year of 1929 when he died in Venice; he astonished petty snobs and women-of-the-world, the broad-minded and the pedantic, litterati and musicians, who were passionate followers of the Ballets Russes.

Diaghilev was a strange character who, although not a painter, dancer or musician, left his mark on the painting, dancing and music of his time. Having been tempted to take up musical composition and dissuaded from his embryonic vocation by Rimsky-Korsakov, he had founded the avant-garde magazine *Le Monde Artiste* and had then established through his collaborators Nourok and Nouvel, the Soirées of Contemporary Music in Saint Petersburg.

In 1909, taking advantage of the Parisian taste for the exotic, and just at the time when Gide was beginning to interpret Dostoïevsky, he presented on the stage of the Théâtre du Châtelet, Chaliapin in *Boris Godounov*, Nijinsky in *Sheherezade*; Ida Rubinstein in *Cleopatra* and finally the dances from *Prince Igor*. It was a bold enterprise, but it met with quite unhoped-for success. The following year, in spite of the financial defection, in desperation, of the Grand Duke Vladimir, Diaghilev carried off with him to Paris a homogeneous company which, under the name of Ballets Russes, were to present, over a period of fifteen years, in all the Western Capitals, creations of Claude Debussy, Maurice Ravel, Igor Stravinsky, Richard Strauss, Sergei Prokofiev, Francis

45

Poulenc, Georges Auric, Henri Sauguet . . .

Thus, in the year 1910, while Feydeau was teaching the Parisians *How to Pot Baby* and while Braque and Picasso were initiating them into the mysteries of cubism, Diaghilev was announcing at the Théâtre du Châtelet, between two performances of *Michel Strogoff*, the *Fire-Bird* of Igor Stravinsky.

1911, 1912, 1913, *Petrouchka, Le Spectre de la Rose, Prélude à l'Après-midi d'un Faune, Daphnis et Chloé* and finally the battle of the *Sacre*. Each year, the fame of the Ballets Russes was spreading. The season would open at Monte-Carlo and then usually continue in London or Paris.

As early as 1895, Sergei Diaghilev had had a presentiment of the part he was destined to play; he wrote to Madame Panaen: 'I think I have found my vocation. Patronage. I have everything necessary for it except money, but that will come!'

Money did come. It brought to light several musical geniuses at the same time as dancers, choreographers, singers and painters. It favoured the flowering of works which dominate the output of this period and the astounding development of the ballet which Diaghilev considered, to the detriment of opera, to be the art-form with the rosiest future.

By his aesthetic ideas and by the productions which he staged, Diaghilev became, in a very short time, one of the most considerable figures in Parisian musical life. His successes were celebrated in Russian avant-garde circles and Prokofiev was not the last to dream of the famous Ballets-Russes season.

Now, in 1914, Sergei Prokofiev had just carried off triumphantly the Rubinstein prize and, to reward him, his mother decided to offer him a trip abroad. Without hesitation, he chose London, where he had spent a short time the previous summer, for the Diaghilev season. The moment was well chosen and Karsavina declared that, during the whole existence of the Ballets Russes, 'the highest peak of success was reached during the summer preceding the war'.

In London, the young man from Saint Petersburg was more than anything impressed by the tall man in dress-suit and top hat, with his monocle and white gloves, whose acquaintance he now made. Diaghilev had heard the *Piano Concerto No. 2* and had been delighted with the score, even envisaging the possibility of using it for a ballet. Prokofiev was unforthcoming in the face of this proposal; he would prefer to entrust to Diaghilev an opera based on *The Gambler* by Dostoïevsky, but the opera was not well received at the Ballets Russes. In the end, the *Concerto No. 2* was not danced and the opera had to wait a few years. On the other hand, Diaghilev suggested to the composer that, on his return to Saint Petersburg, he should write a ballet in collaboration with the symbolist poet Gorodetsky on themes borrowed from the ancient Russian legends. This ballet, after various adventures, earned wide popularity under the title of the *Scythian Suite*.

A few days before the outbreak of hostilities, Prokofiev returned to his

Anna Pavlova

Ballets Russes

Mme Tamar KARSAVINA

country where he was able to escape mobilisation by reason of his family circumstances: his father having died in 1910, he was the only son of a widow. Following the advice of Diaghilev, Prokofiev abandoned for the time being the idea of *The Gambler* and traced with Gorodetsky the main lines of a libretto covering the Scythian period; then, whilst the poet was constructing the plot of the future work, Prokofiev reworked his *Sinfonietta Opus* 5, which he was to conduct at the Ziloti Concerts. Ziloti's invitation was not enthusiastic but, in order to leave no room for doubt as to his gesture's significance, he had written with great frankness in the journal *Music*:

Diaghilev by Larionov

'I do not wish to invite Prokofiev to play his *Concerto No. 2*, because this would oblige me to conduct the orchestra, which is beyond my powers. The music of Debussy exudes perfume, but this stinks. However, since everyone insists, I can invite the composer to conduct his *Sinfonietta*.'

After the Ziloti interlude, Prokofiev occupied himself with the Gorodetsky plans. The poet had been working hard, studying with great application the history of the Scythians but, in compiling the libretto, he came up against serious difficulties, which he overcame painfully with the help of the composer. The composition of the score presented fresh obstacles: Prokofiev's ideas were imprecise; he was still under the spell of the *Sacre du Printemps* which he had recently heard, and wished to 'create a great work'. The emissaries of Diaghilev, Nourok and Nouvel, after a visit to Saint Petersburg, apprised the Master of their misgivings and declared that Prokofiev was 'in the process of giving birth to some crackpot creation on a lunatic subject'. In fact, the composer was worn out with a subject which did not suit him, or of which, at least, he was unaware of the possibilities. The work was long. It was to be interrupted, as a diversion, by the composition of songs, such as the cycle of

At the piano, Nikopol, 1917

the *Ugly Duckling*. Did not Prokofiev repeatedly and freely assert that variety in work was one of his trump cards?

So the gentle little duckling, tender and mocking, was born just as the thunderbolts of the *Scythian Suite* were being let loose! The subject of Andersen's story is familiar: in a nest of ducklings, one is a freak; he is the laughing-stock of the rest and becomes an object of hatred and disgust, persecuted by cocks, turkeys and wild ducks. Autumn and winter only increase his misfortunes; he escapes the ferocity of a hound of the hunt but, when spring comes again, he has gathered enough strength to fly off over a neighbouring pond where he catches sight of three majestic swans, whom he judges worthy to become his executioners: 'Kill me!' he cries to them. At this precise moment, the miracle happens: the water shows him his reflection, that of a marvellous swan. It has pleased some to see autobiographical intentions in this musical account and Gorki, particularly, identified the poor duckling, miraculously transformed, with the author of the score. Outside this interpretation, *The Ugly Duckling* remains a charming work, full of humour and delicacy. The initial version is scored for voice and piano; it was orchestrated later, twice, but in such a way that the vocal part remains perfectly comprehensible. The story is not a mere pretext for the music; it constitutes the very core of the work.

Stravinsky at Biarritz in 1921

At the beginning of the year 1915, Diaghilev was in Rome; he asked Prokofiev to join him and organised a concert for him at the Augusteum, where the *Concerto No. 2* met with a decided success. It was the first appearance of the Russian composer on a foreign platform. The concert was followed by long conversations between the two artists. Diaghilev, after hearing the sketches for *Ala and Lolly*—the famous Scythian ballet— declared that he was not satisfied either with the music or with the arrangement, which he regarded as 'too artificial'. He launched Prokofiev into another subject drawn from a collection of Afanassiev's Russian tales; then he drew up a contract for three thousand roubles, accompanying it with the advice: 'Write some music that truly deserves to be called Russian', adding 'In matters of art, you have to learn to hate, otherwise your own music will lose all its personality'.

'But,' retorts Prokofiev, 'that's the way to become narrow-minded. A canon fires from a distance precisely so that its target shall be narrower.'

Stravinsky also joined Diaghilev. Prokofiev was not unknown to the author of *The Rite of Spring*; their names had appeared side by side on a certain concert programme on 6th December, 1914, but the two men, both towering over contemporary Russian music, their paths frequently crossing, always remained 'friendly enemies'. In 1913, Prokofiev had declared after the performance of the Introduction to the *Fire-Bird* (piano version) that there was no music in the work, or what little there was had been drawn from *Sadko*. This severe judgment had provoked the fury of Stravinsky, who was not disposed to forget the affront. However, the 1915 interview was more cordial; the two composers played *Petrouchka* as a duet at an avant-garde concert and Stravinsky readily praised the merits of the *Concerto No. 2*. Finally, after a brief stay in Italy, Prokofiev returned to Russia and undertook to compile the new ballet which Diaghilev had commissioned: *The Story of a Buffoon who tricked Seven Others*. The work, entitled in Russian *Chout*, is known in English as *The Buffoon*. The plot, based on a popular legend about the Government of Perm, is at once absurd and cruel:

Once, there was a clown.

The clown had a wife, the she-clown.

The clown was sitting by the stove trying to invent a good act. The she-clown was washing the floor.

At last the clown hit on an idea. He jumped down from the stove and said:

'Wife, listen to me; there are seven clowns coming here; I shall tell you to lay the table, you will refuse and I shall pretend to kill you. When you fall down, I shall take a whip. At the first stroke, you must make a movement, at the second, you must turn over, at the third, you must get up and lay the table. Then we shall be able to sell our whip at a good price.'

No sooner said than done. The seven clowns arrived; beheld the

miracle and paid three hundred roubles for the whip.

Back at home, the seven clowns decided to try out the whip. They killed their seven wives, then beat them, but none of them came to life.

The widowers, mad with fury, hurried back to the clown to make him pay dearly for his dirty trick. The clown hid his wife and dressed as a woman so as to be taken for his sister. He sat at the wheel and span. The clowns ransacked the house but could not find the culprit. But they saw his sister spinning. They laid hold of her and carried her off.
'She shall be our cook', they said, 'until we find the clown.'

The seven clowns had seven daughters. The time came to marry them. A merchant arrived with two marriage brokers to choose a bride from among them. The merchant was very, very rich. What joy! But the daughters of the clowns did not please the merchant. He chose the cook.

The merchant led the young bride into his chamber and she became extremely confused.

She said to her husband:

'My love! I do not feel well. Tie me up in a sheet and lower me out of the window. When I pull on the sheet, hoist me up again.'

The merchant obeyed, tied her up in a sheet and let her down through the window. But when he pulled the sheet up again, there was a goat struggling in it.

The merchant was very frightened. He called for help:

'Hurry, good people! My wife has turned into a goat!'

So they hurried to the spot. They tried to break the spell, they shook the goat, and turned it round and round until it collapsed and died.

The merchant, inconsolable, began to bury his wife. At one bound, the clowns leaped over the hedge grimacing and jeering:

'You chose a cook, so much the worse for you!'

Suddenly, the clown appeared and with him seven soldiers.

'Dog, what have you done! Where is my sister?'

They brought him the goat.

The clown seized the merchant by the beard:

'You have taken away my sister and look what you give me back, a dead goat! I'll have you jailed!'

The merchant, terrified, paid three hundred roubles to free himself. And the clown made merry with the she-clown on the merchant's money, whilst the soldiers amused themselves with the daughters of the clowns.[1]

Chout (*The Buffoon*), a thirty-five minute symphonic score, is the first important work in which the composer uses a large orchestra without a soloist. In this way, the work makes it possible to isolate certain characteristic elements of Prokofiev's style which, clearly stated at the time of the *Scythian Suite*, will continue to form the very substance of his future work.

Richness of melody affords one of the keys to the charm of *The Buffoon*. We know that Prokofiev was never separated from his 'notebook of themes', a vast reservoir of melodic material, seemingly inexhaustible because constantly renewed. In fact, Prokofiev's approach to composition was mainly of a melodic order; the construction of a work, research into rhythm and harmonies, the instrumental make-up, were always preceded by the invention of original melodies which in large measure conditioned the realisation of the work. Later on, Prokofiev made a principle of this primary importance of themes, which is in fact the consequence of his extraordinary gift for melody. What contemporary musician could rival Sergei Prokofiev in this field? Perhaps Darius Milhaud. But when considering the composer's melodic invention the

[1]Originally, the clown played tricks on the Priest and his wife as well, but Prokofiev omitted this passage so that the ballet should not be considered, according to Nestiev, 'an anticlerical satire'.

name of one classical composer comes to mind, that of Joseph Haydn, for the themes of these two composers and their spontaneous flow do, if one keeps a sense of proportion, show a certain likeness.

Certainly, treated as a *leitmotif*, Prokofiev's melody is simple, short, often diatonic. Sometimes it wavers between the nostalgic and the witty and resembles a pirouette, like the Clown theme in *The Buffoon*.

Let us look again at the score; from the first bar, we are struck by the ingenious and original use of a densely-instrumented orchestra; this orchestra, with just about two exceptions—the tenor saxophone and the cornet—is identical with that for *Lieutenant Kizhe*, composed twenty years later. It is amusing to compare these two works, both created in Russia, but one in the reign of the last of the Tsars and the other under the Communist régime, and to place them in the same perspective. Indeed, these two scores spring from the same kind of burlesque parody; thus the wedding march of *Kizhe* and the burial correspond to the funeral march accompanying the death of the women in *The Buffoon*. There is another similarity in the inspiration derived from folklore. Russia is evoked with the same felicity in the Dances of the Girls from *The Buffoon* and in the Troika from *Lieutenant Kizhe*. Prokofiev himself explained that he wished to handle *The Buffoon* in a truly Russian spirit: 'In my childhood,' he said, 'I often heard at Sonsovka the young girls of the village regaling us with their songs on a Saturday evening or on Sunday. I do not know whether the region of Sonsovka is poor in popular songs or whether the manner of these village singers, who were not sparing of their voices, irritated me, but whatever the case I did not recognise in these songs any of the beauties of folk-singing and not one of the melodies remained in my memory. I am therefore inclined to think that my subconscious mind retained them; to this I owe the fact that I have been able to master with great ease the truly Russian material in my music. It was as if I had made contact with eternity or sown seed on virgin soil and found an unexpected fruit springing from the unworked earth.'

Melodic flow, instrumental invention, the abundance of comic detail, these are the trump cards of *The Buffoon*. But the success of the work is far from being unanimously recognised and some critics have roundly attacked its 'perpetual mockery', its absence of true lyricism. These reproaches closely resemble a prosecution in Court, for the subject of the *Buffoon* like that of *Lieutenant Kizhe* in no way calls for the outpourings of *Cinderella* or *Romeo and Juliet*; moreover, the only lyrical moments in the *Andante* of the *Buffoon Disguised as a Woman*, emphasised by discreet final dissonances, are, on the contrary, designed to accentuate the comic aspect of the situation.

The first performance of *The Buffoon* took place in Paris in 1921. On the 17th May, the ballet was included in the programme of the Ballets Russes, with décor by Larionov. Three other works accompanied the production: The *Fire-Bird*, the *Quadro Flamenca*, an Andalusian song and dance suite with décor by Picasso and the dances from *Prince Igor*. The reception was highly favourable and M. Roland-Manuel, critic of *L'Eclair*, wrote: '*The Buffoon*, at least where the music is concerned, is the most important work the Russians have produced for us since the war, apart from the admirable *Nightingale* of Monsieur Stravinsky'.

The reception accorded him by Parisians was reciprocally appreciated by Prokofiev, who returned them the eulogies they deserved: '*Here*' (in Paris), he said, 'the public is refined, advanced and knows how to turn the pages skilfully, not only of scores, but of music in general. Diaghilev, who travels in various countries, always arranges that the first performance of any work takes place in Paris, for he thinks that Paris sets the tone.'

Cross–channel critics do not deserve such praise. 'Few composers would think of writing long scores as poor in ideas and as primitive in technique as *The Buffoon* of Prokofiev', wrote Ernest Newman in the *Sunday Times* and Prokofiev replied: 'English critics are the most impolite in the world and I think only the Americans can equal them . . . The musical world of London is far more conservative than that of Paris . . .'

France seems to have been the only champion in the defence of *The Buffoon*, for a German critic declared, after a performance in 1928: 'This Soviet music (sic!) holds all laws in contempt, declares war on all the rules and pushes aside all accepted methods . . . We are plunged into an abyss of monstrous dissonance, a storm of raucous sound, restless and harsh, without the slightest connection. He is mad.'

Finally, this 'Soviet' music was vigorously condemned by Nestiev, the mouth-piece of Russian musical orthodoxy, who discovered in *The Buffoon* 'the grotesque pushed beyond the limits of the permissible', 'a profound and incurable pessimism', 'the laying bare of the stupidity and cruelty of the Russian peasant', 'brawls, murders, the forced presentation of the *canaille*'.

Thirty years later, current opinion appears to support the judgment of the critic of *L'Eclair* . . .

The *Scythian Suite* can be considered as the 'counterbalance' of *The Buffoon*, or, better, its opposite. Three symphonic works, more or less contemporary, represent the poles of Prokofiev's work: the first, *The Buffoon*, is the incarnation of the smiling or sarcastic Prokofiev; the second, the *Scythian Suite*, reveals the powerful savagery of the composer; the third, the *Violin Concerto No.* 1, shows us a sensitive, lyrical musician. In the second work, the rhythmic element is predominant, whilst the melody forms the scaffolding of the two others. So, at the age of twenty-five, Prokofiev had assembled an admirable trilogy. The virtuoso pianist of the Rubinstein Competition was proving his mastery of orchestration and the diversity of his genius. In Russia, war was raging and Revolution was imminent, but Pokofiev never stopped composing . . .

We must remember that the *Scythian Suite* was originally the ballet *Ala and Lolly*, conceived under the driving force of Diaghilev and then rejected by him. After he had finished *The Buffoon*, Prokofiev re-read *Ala and Lolly*, found a certain merit in it and had the idea that a reworking of the piece might well result in a symphonic suite. So the Suite was born which impresarios christened 'the dearest work in the world': indeed, its orchestration is even more brilliant and more dense than that of *The Buffoon*; Prokofiev has reinforced his instrumental reserves with eight hunting-horns, five trumpets and various percussion instruments, but the orchestral sumptuousness, by no means gratuitous, finds its justification in the subject of the work.

The *Scythian Suite* is divided into four tableaux: The *Invocation of Ala and Weles*; *The God of Evil and the Pagan Dance of the Spirits of the Underworld*; *Night*; *Battle of Lolly and Sunrise*. Ala and Lolly are two mythological heroes of the Scythian people, a nation who lived by the Black Sea and whose history is recounted by Herodotus.

Tchoujbog, God of Evil, aided by seven subterranean monsters, desires Ala, a wood-nymph, daughter of Weles, the God of the Sun. But Lolly flies to her rescue and wins the day thanks to the intervention of Weles, who has brought out the sun and rendered Tchoujbog 'hors de combat'.

When Prokofiev wrote the first bars of *Ala and Lolly* he was just back from London where he had heard *The Rite of Spring* and, although Assafiev declared in 1916 in *Music* that: 'Compared with the *Scythian Suite* of Prokofiev, *The Rite of Spring* is simply exotic stuff, the effort of a strange, refined, slightly effeminate European to assimilate unfamiliar impressions', it is obvious that the *Rite*, that great thunderclap which had shaken the music of the time, had deeply impressed the author of the *Scythian Suite*; without the *Rite*, the *Scythian Suite* might have taken on a quite different aspect.

In the two scores, we can perceive the same intensity in the orchestral development, particularly the same predominance of the rhythmic element; however, whereas the complex rhythmic patterns of the *Rite,* brought to light in recent studies, are entirely new in our musical world and thereby the origin of later developments, the rhythm of the *Scythian Suite* is solely a question of dynamism, often an immoderate dynamism. The first movement actually bears the indication *Allegro feroce* and the last *Tempestuoso*. Nevertheless, this evocation of the Scythians is not all wildness: strings, woodwind and piano recreate marvellously the engulfing sensation of *Night*, and a flute sounding over a tremor of violins evokes the enchantment worked by Weles.

Prokofiev himself conducted the first performance of the *Scythian Suite* on 29th January, 1916, at the Mariensky Theatre in Saint Petersburg. Like *The Rite of Spring* the *Scythian Suite* let loose somewhat of a public uproar and Glazounov, who left the hall ostentatiously before the end of the concert, condemned the new work without appeal. Prokofiev described the atmosphere of the concert in a few lines which might have been signed Hector Berlioz:

'The timpanist split the drum with his violent blows and Ziloti promised to send me the lacerated skin as a souvenir. The orchestra itself betrayed certain obstructive symptoms: "It's really only because I have a wife and three children that I submit to this inferno", said the 'cellist into whose ears the trombones behind were blaring terrifying chords. Ziloti, in an excellent mood, walked up and down the hall, repeating: "A slap in the face! A slap in the face!" as much as to say that he would willingly have slapped the audience on Prokofiev's behalf.'

Some months later, there was an announcement of a performance of the *Scythian Suite* in Moscow; at the last moment the concert was postponed, but Sabaneïev, the declared enemy of Prokofiev (he had affirmed that if one opened Prokofiev's body one would find sawdust instead of a soul) wrote in *News of the Moscow Season* a virulent article on the *Suite*, asserting moreover that the composer had conducted with the 'passion of a savage'. However, at the beginning of the autumn season, the work finally entered the repertory. On the 29th April, 1921 Sergei Koussevitsky conducted the first Paris performance in one of a series of three concerts devoted to Russian music. It is sufficient to emphasise that, although the majority of French critics maintained a prudent reserve in the face of the unknown young composer's work, Monsieur Roland-Manuel had the distinction of recognising right away 'a personality of undoubted genius'.

Two-and-a-half years after having, thanks to the *Scythian Suite*, discovered the young Prokofiev, Parisians attended the first performance of the *Violin Concerto in D major* at the Opéra, where the soloist was Marcel Darrieux under the direction of Sergei Koussevitsky. This work, finished in 1917 (the first sketches were dated 1915) represents, as has already been stressed, a lyrical interlude in the composer's output. In this *Violin Concerto No. 1* Nestiev rightly heard 'the vibration of all the joy of living, all the love of sunshine and nature'. The lyrical flow is here controlled by a strongly constructed classic shape (three movements: *Andantino* in the form of an allegro sonata; *Scherzo* and *Moderato*). However, it is not all effusion. A mocking 'smile' seems sometimes to slip furtively in, evoked, for instance, in the theme for bassoon at the beginning of the third movement, which heralds the 'grandfather' *leitmotif* in *Peter and the Wolf*. By reason of its classic form, the expressive virtuosity of the solo part, the skill of its clear, well-balanced orchestration, the *Violin Concerto No. 1 in D major* took its place, from that moment on, in the line of great concertos, enriching a repertoire which violinists rightly estimated to be too restricted.

Between 1915 and 1917, that is round about his twenty-fifth year, Prokofiev was literally devoured by the passion for composition. He attacked every kind of music with equal delight, working simultaneously on the creation of radically different scores. The symphonic trilogy was completed by the very famous *Classical Symphony*, whilst the piano inspired the *Visions Fugitives* and the *Sonatas Nos. 3 and* 4. For voice there was the opera *The Gambler*, several song cycles and the Cantata *They are seven*. Prokofiev was using sheet after sheet of manuscript paper in dizzy succession. 'I would blacken about ten pages of manuscript a day,' he wrote; 'in the easy passages, I would cover as many as eighteen. My mother had occasion to ask Tcherepnin how much music he composed a day. "Sometimes no more than a single chord", he replied, wishing to inspire respect by his minute attention to detail. "My son writes eighteen pages a day!" announced my mother with pride.'

It should be borne in mind that the composer paid hardly any attention to the march of events during the bloody years of 1916 and 1917. To the outbreak of revolution he responded with a short Cantata: *They are Seven*, for dramatic tenor, choir and full orchestra, based on the text of a 'chaldean prayer for the exorcism of demons, cut in cuneiform characters on the walls of an Assyrian temple' and revised by Balmont. The violence of the Cantata recalls the wild accents of the *Scythian Suite* and its 'revolutionary' content is later to be judged ill-suited to the Soviet dogma of realism, since the work 'proves eloquently that the composer had understood nothing in any real sense of the events he had witnessed'. No doubt.

Youthful passion presented Prokofiev with nothing but cares, musically speaking. The 'problem' tackled in creating the *Classical Symphony* was not imitation or pastiche of the old masters, but the possibility of composing a score without the aid of the piano: 'I passed the summer of 1917,' writes Prokofiev in his autobiography, 'in the most complete solitude, in the environs of Petrograd; I read Kant and worked hard. I had deliberately left my piano in town, wishing to try to compose without its help; I had to recognise that thematic material composed without the piano is, for the most part, of higher quality . . . I conceived the plan of composing the whole of a symphonic work without using the piano. In such a work, the orchestral coloration must also be more precise and clear. So I conceived the plan of a symphony in the style of Haydn because, as a result of my classwork under Tscherepnin, Haydn's technique had come to seem particularly clear and this familiarity gave me more confidence to hurl myself, without piano, into these perilous waters. Finally, the title chosen must be a gesture of defiance to enrage the stupid, in the secret hope that I could not but gain by it if, with the passage of time, the symphony should really be confirmed as classical.'

So Prokofiev's intention was not to compose,a pastiche of Haydn, but the Symphony which Haydn would, in his opinion, have written had he lived in the twentieth century. However, the influence of the author of the *Russian Quartets* has here a Slav tinge and a clear analogy has been drawn between the theme in A major of the *Finale* and the *Snegourotchka* air of Rimsky-Korsakov.

The *Classical Symphony* is written for a Haydn or Mozart-type orchestra: flutes, oboes, clarinets, bassoons, trumpets and horns in twos, timpani and strings. The notation is light, concise, transparent and varied with sharp modulations welded into the elegance of the melodic lines. The first movement, in the form of a Sonata Allegro, is constructed on two themes of great freshness,

whereas the second movement, *Larghetto*, whose theme is no less ravishing,

is marked by a gentle poetry, with accents of a truly Mozartian grace. Then the third movement, a heavy-measured *Gavotte*, seated solidly on its four beats,

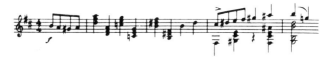

precedes a furious *Finale* which makes some use of the thematic elements of the initial *Allegro*.

The *Classical Symphony* is dedicated to Assafiev, who, under the pseudonym of Glebov, ceaselessly championed his friend's new works. The symphony was performed for the first time under the direction of the composer in Petrograd on 21st April, 1918. On that occasion the public, critics and other musicians were delighted by the charm of the *Symphony* and, in 1927, Florent Schmitt remarked in *La Revue de France*:

'The *Classical Symphony* is an enchantment; a sort of unpublished Mozart, it possesses all his grace, fluidity, and divine perfection; and the orchestration streams out in crystal jets. It would be impossible to achieve a pastiche with more ingenuity or science. For in the case of Monsieur Prokofiev, the complete artist, knowledge equals imagination.'

Before tackling the *Classical Symphony*, Prokofiev had finished the orchestration of his first important opera, *The Gambler*, based on Dostoïevsky; for a long time the composer had wanted to write an opera on this subject, but it will be remembered that the project had been held up because of Diaghilev's reservations. However, after having himself adapted Dostoïevsky's story, Prokofiev wrote the score during the autumn of 1915, in five-and-a-half months, finishing the orchestration during the summer of 1916; he worked with all the more frenzy since he had an early performance in mind. In fact Coates, the English orchestra leader attached to the Mariensky Theatre in Petrograd, had decided to mount the opera although the theatre committee was reticent. A contract was signed.

Alas, the performances of Prokofiev's operas were always pursued by misfortune. *The Gambler*, too, met its set-backs and did not earn the honour of stage production until thirteen years after its completion. What were the reasons for this extraordinary delay? First of all, during the rehearsals at the Mariensky Theatre, the singers and instrumentalists, finding the score too difficult, made it imperative to postpone the date of the première; then, as events grew more serious, the production was abandoned altogether and, when Prokofiev left Russia in May 1918, he left the score behind him in Petrograd. He was able to retrieve it ten years later and the opera was presented for the first time on 29th April, 1929, on the stage of the Théâtre de la Monnaie in Brussels, in a considerably modified version.

In *The Gambler*, Prokofiev was reacting against certain dramatic conventions and endeavouring to impose a new rhythm, create a 'supple, active, touching' opera. He had already proceeded along these lines in cutting the libretto, abandoning the traditional verse form; to the usual arias he preferred 'a conversational style'. The score, vital, nervous, dynamic, skilfully characterising each personage and each situation, responds to this demand.

In support of this, the composer has, moreover, declared his ideas on opera:

Manuscript of 'The Gambler'

'It has been clear,' he says, 'for some years that Russian opera composers are interesting themselves less and less in the theatrical aspect
of the work, and this is giving birth to musical dramas fixed in a
statuesque rigidity and weighed down with a thousand tiresome conventions. . . . For my part, I wanted to give particular attention to the
suppleness of dramatic action. . . . I consider that the habit of writing
operas on rhymed texts is nothing but an utterly absurd convention.
Dostoïevsky's prose is more colourful, possesses more relief and conviction than any poetry. . . .'

Nevertheless, poetry did sometimes inspire Prokofiev:

> '*Tout ce qui est fugitif me fait voir des mondes*
> *Qui dans leur jeu chatoyant*
> *Ont pour moi la valeur du transitoire.*'

These three lines of Balmont provided Prokofiev with the title of his
Visions Fugitives. This collection of twenty pieces for the piano was
assembled after the composition of *Sarcasms*, between 1915 and 1917 and
the order of the pieces 'is not in conformity with that of their origin but
was dictated by artistic considerations'.

The style of these very short scores is particularly varied. The composer displays all the resources of his piano writing and, as a supreme
refinement, deliberately purifies his expression so as to achieve an effect
of true sobriety:

further on, come the well-pointed rhythms so dear to the author of the
Suggestion diablolique, whose echoes can be caught in the 14th *Vision*,
entitled *Féroce*, or in some bars of the 4th piece:

The author of *Schut* and the *Sarcasms* here introduces a biting, witty
turn of phrase:

63

Finally, he sometimes inserts passages of freshness and grace; in these three bars from the second *Vision*, one can see the characteristic use of dotted notes:

The 19th *Vision fugitive* evokes the first battles of the Revolution and plunges us into a bloody reality which the artist had not the leisure to ignore. In fact, in 1917, when the German armies were pushing towards Petrograd, Prokofiev decided to rejoin his mother, who was taking a cure at Kislovodsk; but events were precipitate; news of the most contradictory order arrived in Kislovodsk as to the formation of a Government under Lenin and soon, against his fervent wishes, Prokofiev was no longer able to think of leaving for Petrograd where any plans for a concert would in any case have been vain. Near Rostov, the front was forming under General Kaledin and the town of Kislovodsk was more or less blocked. Prokofiev had just finished the Cantata *They are Seven* and was to remark later on, revealingly: 'I had no work to look forward to and I was bored.' The composer's friends have always laid emphasis on his method, which consisted in fixing plans for work several months in advance, so as not to allow himself any respite. 'It was impossible for him,' says Shostakovitch, 'not to compose every day, and the days when he had to "rest" were for him the most painful ones.'

This boredom did not last long; in March 1918, the Kaledin front surrendered and, within a week, Prokofiev was able to regain Moscow, having prudently provided himself with a pass supplied by the workers' Soviet of Kislovodsk. His journey to the capital enabled him to sign an important contract, involving six million roubles, with Koussevitsky, but it seems that the offer was not disinterested: it consisted of money which rapidly devalued, in exchange for work the value of which could only increase. The publishers will retort that Prokofiev was not always fired by the best of intentions in their regard . . .

During this same stay, the composer also encountered the poet Mayakovsky, who presented him with *War and the Universe* with the famous dedication: 'To the President of the Musical Section of the Universe—the President of the Poetry Section of the Universe, Mayakovsky.'

At the beginning of the year 1918, in spite of the uncertainty of the political situation, musical life slowly began to pick up in Petrograd; on the 15th April, Prokofiev gave a first performance of the *Visions fugitives* and the *Piano Sonata No. 3*; then, two days later, the *Sonata No. 4*. These two Sonatas had been composed a few months earlier, both 'from the old notebooks', that is to say based on material supplied by the work of extreme youth. An important fragment of the *Sonata No. 4* originates, in particular, from the *Symphony in E Minor* of 1908.

Some days after the execution of the Sonatas, Prokofiev conducted the first performance of the *Classical Symphony*; the People's Commissar for Public Instruction attended the concert, knowing that Prokofiev intended to leave Russia for America. 'You are a revolutionary in music,' he said to him at the end of the evening, 'whereas we are revolutionaries in life. We are made to work hand in hand. However, if you wish to leave, I shall not put obstacles in your way.'

A fortnight later, on 27th May, 1918, Prokofiev left Petrograd behind him. He took with him the thematic material for a *Piano Concerto* and the outline of a libretto for *The Love of Three Oranges*.

Eisenstein's 'October'

Prokofiev, Petrograd 1966. Autograph 'That's right, it's I'

Mayakovsky

Prokofiev and Mayakovsky in Moscow, 1941

Oranges: 43,000 Dollars Each

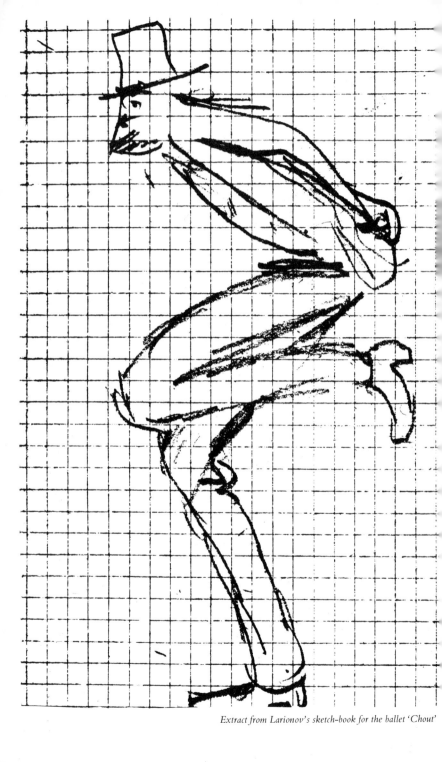

Extract from Larionov's sketch-book for the ballet 'Chout'

ORANGES: 43,000 DOLLARS EACH

Prokofiev only ever had one problem: the working out of his compositions. Beside this necessity, everything else seemed to him of secondary importance. There is no need to look elsewhere for an explanation of his travels and of the decisions which determined a new direction in his life.

Prokofiev left Russia in 1918 because it was impossible for him to work peacefully in a country torn by war. The Revolution did not interest him, neither did the Counter-Revolution. He was looking for a refuge where he might continue to compose music. When he returned to his country, fifteen years later, one motive seems likely. The fact is that the financial difficulties which he had encountered in the West prevented him from composing as much as he would have liked and forced him to undertake frequent tours and recitals. It had been intimated to him during the course of his journey to Russia in 1927 that the Soviet artist, free of material cares, was able to devote all his time to the creation of his work. And, indeed, from 1940 onwards, Prokofiev was able to abandon his career as virtuoso pianist.

Subsequently to this decision, when one of his friends was trying to persuade him to give a special recital, he refused in these significant terms: 'No, it would cost me half a sonata!'

Let us go back to the year 1918. Prokofiev had left Petrograd. A journey lasting eighteen days, during which he read attentively a book on Babylon, careless of the dangers surrounding him, brought him to

Vladivostok. He was hoping to get to South America and was studying Spanish but, since there was no ship going to those parts, he changed plans and embarked for San Francisco via Japan and Honolulu. In Japan, he had to wait two months for an American visa, and this enabled him to give three concerts, two at the Imperial Palace in Tokyo and one at Yokohama. Finally, he disembarked at San Francisco, whence he made his way rapidly to New York.

Five months had passed since the departure from Petrograd, but this time was not to be wasted by a creative nature as ardent as Prokofiev's, for 'the length of the journey, the encounter with new countries and new people, had had not the slightest repercussion on his creative work and he had found the time . . . to compose the themes and draw up the plan for *The Love of Three Oranges*' (Nestiev). This might signify power of detachment, or lack of interest in anything but musical questions.

On his arrival in the United States, Prokofiev was surprised by musical customs of which he had had no experience in Russia. In his country, everything was geared to the polemics of new artistic trends. Here, on the other hand, musical life was centred upon the executant. The cult of the interpreter relegated the composer to second place. However, the New York public, attracted by a 'bolshevik' musician, thronged to the first recital, given on 20th November, 1918. The reception was moderate and some press excerpts did not lack bite: The *Finale* of the *Sonata No.* 2 'recalls the charge of a herd of mammoths on an Asian plateau' declared one reviewer.

Prokofiev was the 'Titan pianist' or the 'Mendelssohn with false notes' and the critic of *Musical America* offered the following as a recipe:

'Take one Schoenberg, two Ornsteins, a little Satie, mix with some Medtner, add a drop of Schumann, then a shade of Scriabin and Stravinsky, and you will have a cocktail resembling the music of Prokofiev.'

Finally, it appeared that the pianist's style lacked 'nuances', but it was acknowledged that 'the fingers are of steel, the wrists are of steel, the biceps and triceps are of steel'.

Despite this not very encouraging humour, American publishers became interested in this 'barbarian'. A commission enabled him to compose *Les Contes de la Vieille Grand'mère* and the *Gavotte, Opus* 32. One firm even proposed that he should have his work recorded for a piano-player.

So the *Contes de la Vieille Grand'mère* were to be the first pages written on American soil. The four pieces are characterised by a discreet lyricism and a real freshness of inspiration: a simple melody, rather like a folk song, is sustained by a transparent harmony. But plans to publish fell through. The author would not accept the poor financial terms proposed. A new contract for two or three years to do concert tours met with hardly more success. Prokofiev avoided committing himself for the immediate future. Perhaps he was thinking of a prompt return to Russia.

In the meantime, he appeared in New York at a second concert, to perform, under the direction of an undistinguished Russian conductor, Modest Altschuler, his *Piano Concerto No.* 1. This work which, as will be remembered, unleashed some lively protest at the time of its creation in Moscow, now underwent further attack from the critics. One launched the following, which will make a nice contribution to the collection of inanities to be found in musical history: 'If that is music, I really believe I prefer agriculture!'

Another critic affirmed: 'Prokofiev is the Cossack Chopin of future generations.'

Justifiably disappointed by New York's reception, the composer tried his luck in Chicago. There, under the direction of the percipient conductor, Frederick Stock, the *Concerto No.* 1 and the *Scythian Suite* enjoyed a positive success. According to the *Daily News*: '. . . Russia is administering the antidote to French impressionism which, with its delicate light and shade, so flattering to the ear, impregnated the whole of European music before the war.' And a journal of the extreme Left hailed with enthusiasm the 'representative of Revolutionary Russia'.

Very soon, Prokofiev's fame had spread in Chicago to such an extent that the Director of the Opera, the Italian Campanini, suggested the performance of one of his operatic works. The score of *The Gambler* having unfortunately been left behind in Petrograd, it was proposed to create an opera on Gozzi's *The Love of Three Oranges*. 'Gozzi, our dear friend Gozzi, but that is marvellous!' cried Campanini, won over by the name of his illustrious compatriot and, in January 1919, the contract was signed. The work to be ready the following autumn.

Three years previously, Prokofiev had completed *The Gambler*. In what spirit was he now to tackle a work whose story and atmosphere were so radically different?

'Taking into account the American mood(!),' he says, 'I chose a musical language much simpler than that of *The Gambler* and the work made speedy progress. The stage play appealed to me enormously. The novelty resided in the three different planes on which the action unfolded itself: the first, that of the characters in the story (the Prince, Truffaldino and the others); the second, that of the forces of the underworld (to which belong the Fairy Morgana and the Magician Celio); the third, that of the Comics, who are in a way emissaries, commenting on the action.'

Gozzi's play, inspired by an Italian fairy tale which Prokofiev had probably known during the war[1] through a group of young artists who had published a magazine with just that title: *The Love of Three Oranges*, has a biting humour and a lightness which immediately attracted the composer.

Count Carlo Gozzi was a Venetian dramatist of the eighteenth century, whose punctillious nature is reflected in his *Useless Memoires*. He was fiercely opposed to Carlo Goldoni, reformer of the Italian theatre, who had substituted written and character comedy for the Commedia dell'Arte; but the plays of Gozzi, by their fantasy and verve, outclassed those of his rival. *The Love of Three Oranges* draws on an episode from these literary battles and is in the tradition of the Commedia dell'Arte. The satire is evident in the first tableau of the second Act, when Truffaldino discovers in the Prince's cuspidor certain 'striking rhymes'. The Comics explain: he is fed on 'martellian' verse (i.e. by

[1]*Contemporary Music,* Moscow 1927.

Pier Jacopo Martelli, an indifferent poet who had introduced the Alexandrine into Italian poetry).

In the play are encountered the characters of the Commedia dell'Arte and of the 'fabias' of Gozzi (fabia—fable-play), i.e. Pantaloon, Truffaldino, Leander, Clarissa and so on. A literary satire at a time when intellectual circles in Russia were aflame with this sort of discussion could not have been uninteresting to Prokofiev. Moreover, a subject inspired by the Italian Commedia dell'Arte was no stranger to Russian music. Victor Balaeff has justly emphasised that 'the Italian element has deep roots in Russian musical psychology, for:

1. The first masters of Russian musicians were Italian composers;
2. Russia, until the end of the last century, has made use in popular spectacles for the Lent Carnival of the traditions of the Commedia dell'Arte which, as is well known, enjoyed huge popularity in Western and Eastern Europe during its peak period'.[1]

The opera begins with a short prologue showing the Choir divided into Tragics, Comics, Lyrics, Empty-Heads and 'Ridicules'. These various groups are to comment on the action and even intervene in it during the third Act. During the Prologue they engage in close combat to champion their theatrical theories, then the curtain parts on a set representing the Royal palace.

A melancholy Prince and a solemn King, his father, are the central figures of the comedy. The plot is thickened by the presence of sorcerers and magicians, of the wicked Clarissa, niece of the King who, aided by a Minister, plots the death of the Sovereign and, of course, of three oranges concealing three ravishing princesses. The Prince will not recover from his hypochondria until the day he can smile; the Clowns do their best, but in vain, and Truffaldino, the Prince's valet, does no

[1]The thematic work was undertaken immediately.

better, whilst the wicked Minister Leander slyly boasts of having slipped some 'martellian' verses into the Prince's bread and cut some up for his soup so as to delay his recovery. But the Fairy Morgana, Queen of Hypochondria, accidentally makes the Prince laugh. The young man is cured, but the Fairy Morgana, in fury, weaves an evil spell over him: he must fall in love with three oranges for whom he must search unceasingly.

After some fantastic adventures, the Prince and Truffaldino come to the desert; they have just discovered the three oranges at the home of the 'terrible' Créonte. While his master is sleeping, the thirsty valet cannot resist opening one of the oranges. A wonderful young maiden, the Princess Linette, emerges, faints away immediately and dies of thirst. The second orange and the second Princess, Nicolette, meet the same fate. Truffaldino, out of his mind, takes flight. The Prince then wakes up, opens the third orange and out comes the Princess Ninette. She is on the point of dying, but the 'Ridicules' bring a bucket of water just in time and the Prince and Princess are able to unite their hearts in a beautiful love duet. But all is not yet spoken. The negress Smeraldina, inspired by the Fairy Morgana, transforms Ninette into a rat and takes her place at the Prince's side. Just at the moment when the marriage of the Prince to Smeraldina is to be celebrated, there is the inevitable *coup de théâtre*. Ninette appears on the throne in her rat's disguise and the good magician Celio uses his supernatural powers to break the charm. The wicked are put to flight, the good are rewarded, the comedy ends happily. . . .

Prokofiev himself wrote the libretto of the Opera in French, in collaboration with Vera Janacopoulos. His text often takes on a satirical, even a farcical tone. Thus, the Prince declares his love to Ninette, crying: 'I have conquered the abominable cook, I have braved the vile mortal, I have passed through the inferno which is her kitchen. No, my love is stronger than Créonte, more fiery than the kitchen!'

The musical score effects a sort of compromise between *Chout* and the *Classical Symphony*. It abandones certain over-rich orchestral excesses whilst preserving a wit and bite which recall the charm of *Chout*. The orchestration, always ingenious, is of such clarity that the declamation quite naturally takes the predominant place; it is light and lively, and preserves a perfect balance between voice and instruments. The lyricism of the love duet must be emphasised. According to R. Hofmann, it 'anticipates the finest pages of Romeo'. There are those who try to claim that lyricism is absent from Prokofiev's work. The rarity of its appearance in his youthful compositions is more indicative of a reticence of expression than of dryness of sentiment. It is as a reaction against impressionism, and also in order to keep to the way of Stravinsky and the Ballets Russes, that Prokofiev avoids at that time any long effusive passages. But pieces like the duet from *The Love of Three Oranges* or certain fragments from the *Violin Concerto No. 1* prove that the composer's nature is already full of a lyricism which is merely waiting to express itself.

The career of *The Love of Three Oranges* followed a wayward course. As he was composing it, Prokofiev had suddenly fallen ill and had completed the score only with difficulty. On the 1st October, 1919, however, it was finished, and the rehearsals were able to start. But three months later, Campanini, Director of the Chicago Opera, died suddenly and the production was postponed to a later date. The following year, Prokofiev, in association with the new Director, claimed compensation from the fact that the work had not been mounted at the date envisaged, but the contract was not sufficiently explicit and the composer's demands were left unconsidered.

In 1921, interest was renewed. The directoral chair at the Chicago Opera welcomed a *directress with generous gestures*, Mary Garden, the unforgettable creator of *Pelléas and Mélisande*. The rehearsals of *The Love of Three Oranges* began at once under the attentive direction of the composer and the first night, on 30th December, 1921, was hailed as a great success. The cast, although somewhat disparate, was enhanced by the presence of the great singer, Nina Kochitz, in the rôle of the Fairy Morgana.

Hoping to transform this success into a triumph, the Chicago Opera presented the work in New York on 14th February of the same year. Prokofiev, who had given a recital a few hours before, directed the orchestra. The public was delighted with Gozzi, Prokofiev, Truffaldino and the Fairy Morgana, but the critics, unwilling to allow Chicago, the rival city, to carry off a New York success, expressed their hostility in terms which showed a rare lack of understanding. One critic wrote ironically: 'The production cost 130,000 dollars, that is, 43,000 dollars each orange, but the opera displeased us so much that a second performance would be absolutely ruinous.' A second summed up his impressions as follows: 'Fifteen minutes of Russian jazz with some bolshevist flourishes. All very amusing, but two-and-a-half hours—this is really too

77

'The Love of Three Oranges' by the Ljubliana Opera

much!' Finally Deems Taylor declared in *World* that 'Prokofiev's work was a straight disappointment. First of all there is no melody. There are melodic lines, dozens of them, but they lead nowhere.'

Since this double presentation, *The Love of Three Oranges* has all too seldom graced the stage. Mounted in Moscow and in Leningrad in 1927, the opera was then, according to Nestiev, completely and inexplicably abandoned by Russian companies; moreover, although the libretto was written in French, no French operatic management has so far thought of staging Prokofiev's work.

Although the opera may not have benefited from the wide-spread performance it might have expected, its fame is now assured, thanks to the *Orchestral Suite Op.* 33 which the composer has taken from it. The six tableaux (The 'Ridicules', Hell Scene, March, Scherzo, the Prince and the Princess and The Flight) of this skilfully constructed canvas, are frequently executed and the opera itself seems to be swallowed up in their great popularity.

The Love of Three Oranges dominates Prokofiev's American period. This period of four years (1918 to 1922) during which the legendary fecundity of the composer was exposed daily to the difficulties reserved in the United States for a daring, 'barbarous', 'bolshevik' musician, was also marked by the creation of the *Overture on Jewish Themes* and the

Prokofiev's piano transcription of the March from 'The Love of Three Oranges'

Piano Concerto No. 3; several songs and the *Contes de la Vieille Grand'mère*. Prokofiev also sketched, during his years in America, the outlines of the opera *The Flaming Angel*.

In October 1918, a Jewish music ensemble called 'Zimro' arrived in New York. The musicians who had been friendly with Prokofiev in the Saint Petersburg days sent him a notebook of genuine Jewish themes, asking him to compose an Overture for Sextet based on them. To present thematic material to a composer with limitless melodic gifts—what impertinence! Prokofiev refused without hesitation. He did, however, preserve the collection, which he opened negligently some months later; as his hand happened, by chance, to be resting on a keyboard, the Jewish themes were soon adorned with new harmonies. In two days, the *Overture* was completed.

A work has only to have its origins in folk-music and musicologists mistrust it: are the themes really authentic? The inevitable question was raised about the *Overture*. One commentator recently stated: 'Nestiev claims that the themes are genuine; there is nothing in this whatsoever. It is one of Prokofiev's neatest achievements that he should have consistently invented airs which one would swear to be folk tunes, so characteristic are they of the *genre*.' The opposite thesis is to be drawn from the autobiography of the composer. Is it convincing? If there had been any subterfuge, would Prokofiev have admitted its existence in 1943 when the Soviet régime was cracking up the virtues of genuine folklore? The problem is fortunately of secondary importance.

The *Overture* was performed successfully in New York on 26th January, 1920. Scored for clarinet, piano and string quartet, the piece was instrumented by the composer[1] in 1934 for a small symphony orchestra. The second version is without doubt more colourful and the instrumentation, despite its simplicity, adds to its attraction. Dance themes contrast with a long, melancholy melodic line; the rhythmic element creates, by its repetition, the magical atmosphere of an appealing folk-song.

The *Piano Concerto No. 3*, composed two years later, is obviously the great symphonic score of that period; but it owes nothing to America. In fact, it was sketched out in Russia as early as 1916 (the motif of the 2nd movement even dates back to 1913) and completed in France during a summer holiday spent by Prokofiev on a Breton beach.

The *Piano Concerto No. 3*, achieving as it does a perfect balance of poetry and fantasy, violence and charm, and offering a new meaning to traditional forms (the second movement is simply an Andante with variations) is the supreme expression of a *modern* musician who wishes to

[1]Previously, the instrumentation of the *Overture* had been extended several times, principally by Alfred Cortot in preparation for a performance at the Ecole Normale.

be a *classical* one. 'What is a classical composer?' demanded an American journalist of Prokofiev: 'He is a mad creature', replied Prokofiev, 'who composes work incomprehensible to people of his own generation. He has discovered a certain logic, as yet unknown to others, so that they cannot follow him. Only later do the roads he has pointed out, if they are good ones, become understandable to those around him. To write simply according to the rules established by previous classics signifies that one is not a master, but a pupil. Such a composer is easily acceptable by his contemporaries, but has no hope of surviving his own generation.'

Now the *Piano Concerto No. 3*, which departs quite naturally from the revolutionary language of, say, Schoenberg, since Prokofiev never submitted to the temptations of atonal or serial composition, nevertheless springs from a contemporary aesthetic; neither neo-classical nor neo-romantic, it speaks a language of our time which can be admired equally by the most revolutionary musicians or the most timid music-lovers. For Prokofiev masks his new harmonies as skilfully as his borrowings from the old masters. This subtle and dangerously inexplicable balance—originality cannot be explained—sometimes invited comparison with Mozart. And it is indeed nice to think of a Mozart born in the Ukraine in 1891 who would have composed perhaps a little like Prokofiev.

The arrangement of themes and the instrumentation of the *Concerto No. 3* are particularly noteworthy. The latter is a constant outpouring, the former ingenious in its skilful handling. The first movement, a brilliant *Allegro*, is preceded by a short lyrical introduction from which a charming melody emerges on the clarinet:

then the strings introduce the piano, which states a heavily rhythmical first theme:

The second motif, for oboe over pizzicato accompaniment, is expressive, on the other hand, of a delicately humorous sweetness:

The theme of the *Andante with variations* is a long melody with full orchestra:

This *Andante*, rather restrained in its realisation, combines ardour, contrast and colour.

The third movement, *Allegro*, opens with an energetic and persistent theme:

preceding the dreamy intervention of the piano. Finally, a tremendous lyrical surge takes possession of the whole orchestra and the *Concerto* ends in a whirl of sound. The two themes of this *Finale* stem from a *Quatuor blanc* sketched by Prokofiev in 1918 and later abandoned.

From the moment of its creation in Chicago, the *Piano Concerto No. 3* was unanimously acclaimed and considered 'the most beautiful modern concerto for piano' (*Daily Herald*). However, this unanimity was briefly interrupted by the New York public, that same New York public who, inspired by feelings of hostility to Prokofiev—and to Chicago—had earlier on booed *The Love of Three Oranges*. We know that this setback had nothing to do with his talent, and Prokofiev was aware of this, but he was cruelly savaged by the hostility of a certain section of the American public.

'The man with the steel fingers', fêted at the time of his first concerts, was rapidly allowed to fall into neglect. Worse than hostility, indifference now greeted the young composer's work: 'As I wandered in the enormous parks in the centre of New York,' he writes in his

Ansermet, Diaghilev, Stravinsky and Prokofiev

autobiography, 'looking at the skyscrapers which dominated them, I thought with cold rage of the marvellous American orchestras which were not playing my music, of the critics who were repeating over and over again what had already been said, such as: "Beethoven is a composer of genius" and who were brutally thrusting aside anything new, of the impresarios organising long tours for artists who were rendering the same programme of known work fifty times over. I had come here much too soon. "The child" (America) had not grown up sufficiently to accept new music.'

Prokofiev was himself subjected to the exigencies of impresarios, and on his long concert tours across the United States and Canada, he made

4 GRANDS CONCERTS SYMPHONIQUES

SERGE KOUSSEVITZKY

3ᵉ **CONCERT** : En Soirée, le Jeudi 3 Juin 1926
à 21 heures précises

FESTIVAL DE MUSIQUE RUSSE

-:- PROGRAMME -:-

Iʳᵉ PARTIE

1. **Rouslan et Ludmila** (ouverture) .. .. GLINKA

2. **Feu d'Artifice** . .. . STRAWINSKY

3. **Chout** .. .. PROKOFIEFF
   (Fragments de la suite du Ballet)

4. **La Préface du Livre de Vie** .. .. . OBOUHOW
   Iʳᵉ audition

   Mmes LOUISE MATHA, ANNA KERNER
   MM. BASILE BRAMINOW et NARÇON
   Au piano double : **l'AUTEUR** *et* **M. N. SLONIMSKY.**

ENTR'ACTE

5. **Quatrième Symphonie**, *en fa mineur.*
   op. 36 .. .. TCHAIKOWSKY
   1. *Andante sostenuto: moderato con animo*
      (in movimento di valse)
   2. *Andantino in modo di canzona*
   3. *Scherzo; Pizzicato ostinato; Allegro*
   4. *Finale: Allegro con fuoco*

Orchestre de 100 Exécutants sous la Direction de M. Serge KOUSSEVITZKY

PIANO PLEYEL

up his programmes from the *Carnival* of Schumann, the *Preludes* of Rachmaninov or the *Mazurkas* of Chopin, occasionally playing one of his own compositions as an encore.

In 1921, after the setbacks of *The Love of Three Oranges* and the *Piano Concerto No. 3* in New York, things came to a head. 'I had to face facts,' writes Prokofiev, 'this season in America which had begun with such excitement was in the end to gain me nothing.' His decision was taken. Since the Chicago Opera, after the departure of Mary Garden, offered him no encouragement in the composition of *The Flaming Angel* and since American journalists persisted in attributing to him the title of 'performer' only, referring to the 'composer Stravinsky' and the 'pianist Prokofiev', he must leave that inhospitable soil.

Did he for a moment think of returning to Russia? There is no real evidence that he did. But of course, he was attracted by Paris, where he remained in residence after a visit to Germany.

In April 1920, Prokofiev had already left America once for Europe, and the journey had given him the opportunity to meet Diaghilev and Stravinsky. It had also allowed him to detail the plans with regard to the stage production of *Chout* and, on the advice of Diaghilev, the composer installed himself in Mantes for the whole of the summer, to make certain alterations to the ballet. During this same summer, he had also prepared the transcriptions of a Buxtehude Fugue and some of Schubert's waltzes, to fill out the programme of his recitals.

The following year, Paris discovered *Chout*, thanks to Diaghilev, and the *Scythian Suite*, thanks to Koussevitsky. Some months later, Prokofiev finished the *Piano Concerto No. 3* in Brittany. On the whole, France already offered the composer a more welcoming aspect than the United States had done.

All links with the New World being temporarily severed, Prokofiev installed himself in March 1922 at Ettal, a picturesque little German village situated on the slopes of the Bavarian Alps. Ettal was, for eighteen months, a sort of pied-à-terre, a refuge between journeys, and Prokofiev took care to emphasise that he was not in touch with any German musical circles. Already his true magnetic pole was Paris.

Concert tours, performances of his work in European capitals, plans for publication at the house of Koussevitsky, new negotiations with Diaghilev, all this left little time for creative work, and the stay at Ettal produced only a few sketches for *The Flaming Angel* and the composition of the *Piano Sonata No. 5*, a sonata into which crept, particularly in the third movement, certain Eastern influences. What Nestiev calls 'a confused chromatism, an artificially complicated melodic line where "invention" gets the better of true sentiment' does not reveal a new language, but signifies a quest which will be intensified in the later work.

Five years had passed since the departure from Petrograd; five years representing an impressive number of tours and eight new works (besides transcriptions). Material difficulties had certainly impeded, quantitatively, the creative power of the composer, but it would be absurd to judge a musician according to the number of works he produces. To counter certain 'politically slanted' affirmations it is obvious that a period in which *The Love of Three Oranges* and the *Piano Concerto No. 3* were conceived is far from showing a falling-off in Prokofiev's creative power.

In October 1923, Prokofiev left Germany, with which he had hardly formed an acquaintance, and installed himself in Paris.

The Fine Taste of the Parisians

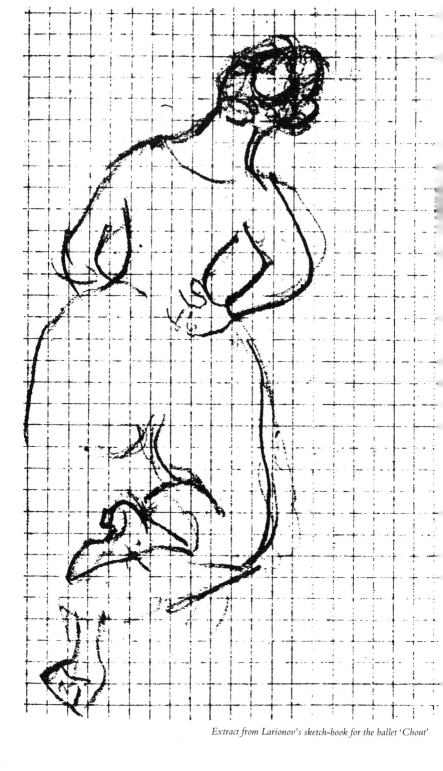

Extract from Larionov's sketch-book for the ballet 'Chout'

THE FINE TASTE OF THE PARISIANS

In 1918, Jean Cocteau declared: 'A poet always has too many words in his vocabulary, a painter too many colours in his palette, a musician too many notes on his keyboard.'

He added: 'The public enquires. It must be answered by work, not by manifestos.'

Work, in fact, emerged slowly. At the end of the war, after a five-year silence, the artistic life of Paris was seeking to define its own features. Among the newcomers eager to make their mark, aesthetic standards remained blurred, but the young were gaining confidence. Solidly supported by Jean Cocteau, the 'New Young' soon became 'The Six'. The future might be a problem, but the past was becoming clear. After brandishing the national flag in opposition to the Wagnerian thunder-bolts, the New Young pursued the struggle, at the same time condemn-ing the anti-Wagner:—Claude Debussy. They refused on principle all music 'listened to head in hand', such as *Tristan* or *Pelléas*. To impose your own taste, you must destroy accepted ones.

The popularity of Wagner was not in the slightest degree affected. Statistics relating to the frequency of appearance on Parisian concert programmes of certain composers during the season 1922 to 1923 reveal that the Master of Bayreuth figures largely at the head with 334 perform-ances of his work, followed by Beethoven with 139; Saint-Saëns with 111; César Franck with 98; Mozart with 76.

By a curious reaction, the young composers who were manifesting

89

such violent opposition to their immediate predecessors were looking for an example (enriched, it is true, by modern experience) from among the old masters; the return to Bach and the economy of linear writing were taking the place of the spell-binding harmonies of *Pelléas*. However, the older generation: Fauré, Ravel, Roussel, Florent Schmidt, were beginning to interest a public still retarded by one generation whilst Stravinsky remained the focus of all avant-garde circles.

On the fringes of creation proper, the musical life of Paris experienced during the post-war period an incomparable burgeoning and splendour. The whole of Europe was represented at the Opéra or at the Théâtre des Champs-Elysées, and the consecration of that capital was not yet an exaggeration. The Ballets Russes had re-opened their season. The splendour of the stage rivalled the luxury of the auditorium, where Academicians, generals, ambassadors, celebrated *femmes du monde* and artists thronged in serried ranks. This same public, answering the call of snobbery and social success, were also to be found at the grand 'premières' of the Ballet Suédois of Rolf de Maré. While Diaghilev and the Russian émigrés were ensuring the success of Slav music, Spain was also setting the tone in this European concert: there were the visits of Albeniz and Manuel de Falla. The Germans and Italians, in their turn, were displaying, albeit rather more discreetly, their Schoenbergs, Hindemiths, Malipieros, Casellas. Exoticism was exciting the curiosity of musicians; not conventional 'chinoiserie and turquerie' but the *Padmavati* of Roussel, the *Salammbô* of Schmitt, the *Saudades* of Milhaud and, later, the *Choros* of Villalobos. Finally, the *Revue Nègre* at the Théâtre des Champs-Elysées hurled the jazz bomb-shell.

This terrible and engulfing Paris was already familiar to Prokofiev when the author of *Chout*, in October 1923, was choosing his new home. But Prokofiev was not taken in. 'Living in Paris,' he said, 'does not yet signify that one is Parisian, and the victorious French wanted to repeat the victory in the world of music; this accounts for the exceptional interest aroused by The Six, an interest which they did not altogether deserve.'

1923: In Paris, musical life is particularly brilliant. The Ballets Russes are showing Stravinsky's *Noces*; the Ballets Suédois are presenting *The Creation of the World*; there is *Padmavati* at the Opera and the Princesse de Polignac has invited her friends to a private performance of the *Retable de Maître Pierre* of Manuel de Falla.

Prokofiev's name also appeared on the posters. His *Piano Concerto No. 1* was performed on 25th February at the Concerts Pasdeloup and, on 20th October, the Concerts Koussevitsky presented the first performance of the *Violin Concerto No. 1*; later, on 5th November, on the stage of the Théâtre des Champs-Elysées, a tall young man with fair hair crossed the short distance from wings to piano with long strides; the 'steel hands' beat on the keyboard and Prokofiev attacked the first bars of a transcription of a Buxtehude *Prelude and Fugue for Organ*; then came one of

Costumes by Léger for the Ballet Suédois

Medtner's *Fairy Tales* and the *Bizarreries* of Miaskovsky; then Prokofiev interpreted by Prokofiev: *opus* 12, *opus* 32 and the *Gavotte from the Classical Symphony*. The evening ended with two Schubert Waltzes. The first Parisian recital by Prokofiev was a success—a triumph in fact. Four months later, in the same Théâtre des Champs-Elysées, Prokofiev performed the *Pictures in an Exhibition* and, for the first time, his own *Piano Sonata No. 5*.

He had forgotten what it was like to be acclaimed as a pianist as well as fêted as a composer. He was only thirty-three years old and the French critics were unanimous in considering him one of the significant musicians of our time. How could he resist the appeal of Paris?

But Paris was never a second mother-country for him. It was simply a point of attachment. From the rue Valentin-Haüy, the rue La Fontaine, the Quai de Passy or from his small suburban flat where he lived with his mother and his wife, he cast a somewhat disdainful glance at the over-sterile antics of the young artists, and the contempt he registered on encountering The Six was dispelled only when he found himself face to face with Francis Poulenc at a bridge table.

After a particularly close game, the author of the *Biches* addressed the score of his *Concert champêtre* to Prokofiev, with the inscription: 'To Sergei Prokofiev, with very few trumps in my hand'. Poulenc, in his modesty, had guessed that his friend Sergei preferred playing bridge with him or spending a week-end at his house in Touraine to listening to his music. Poulenc shared this sad privilege with French musicians in general.

Prokofiev with his first wife Lina Llubera, a singer of mixed Russian and Spanish origin

One day, as he was passing by the Invalides with Nabokov[1] Prokofiev pointed an avenging finger in the direction of the famous canons and said:

'Look how angry they seem. I have the same feeling when I go to a concert in Paris. All those Countesses and Princesses and ridiculous snobs make me furious. They act as though everything in the world had been created to amuse them . . . Look what their "salon" mentality has done to French music. There has been no first-rank French musician since the time of Chabrier and Bizet.'

Prejudice? Or the expression of a personal aesthetic? Prokofiev is pitiless, even towards 'accepted' standards.

For him, Debussy is 'gelatine, absolutely spineless music;' Satie 'a mystifier;' Roussel: 'his Third Symphony is far from uninteresting;' but 'the only composer in France who knows what he is doing is Ravel.'

Prokofiev's vindication is the sincerity of his judgements and the fidelity of his admiration. On the death of Maurice Ravel, he wrote in a Soviet journal:

'A telegram has just informed me of the death of Maurice Ravel. With him is lost one of the greatest composers of our time. It is certain that at present not all musicians take into account the importance of his gifts and of his mastery. Although he followed in the footsteps of Debussy, Ravel has enriched the language of music with a new and personal dowry. For us Soviet musicians it is especially interesting to observe that, like Debussy, Ravel not only expressed a profound interest in Russian Music but came under its influence, first and foremost through Moussorgsky and Rimsky-Korsakov . . . We must regret that the work of Ravel should have been so rarely performed in this country of late by reason of a false notion that his music is foreign to our time. I am prepared to think that such an idea is unjustifiable. . . . My first encounter with Ravel took place in Paris in 1920. It was at a "thé musical" at which Stravinsky and Ansermet were present, among others. Suddenly, there appeared a man of small stature with sharp, well-defined features and rather upstanding hair beginning to turn white. I was told he was Ravel and was introduced to him. When I expressed my delight at shaking the hand of so great a composer, calling him "Maître" (as celebrated artists are addressed in France), he suddenly withdrew his hand, as though I were going to kiss it, and cried: "Please don't call me 'Maître'!" Humility was characteristic of him . . .'

In 1923, Prokofiev was thus the Parisian show-piece; it was essential to

[1]Nabokov. *Old Friends and New Music.*

Ravel bathing at Saint Jean de Luz, by A. Benois

see, hear and receive him. But the composer, irritated by the futility of this worldly comedy, felt some bitterness when the first wave of enthusiasm began to ebb.

'Paris,' he said, 'incontestably dictates the laws of feminine fashion and this interest in fashion spills over to some extent on to other activities. In music, the fine taste of the French has a reverse side, in that it is inconstant. A year or two after taking an interest in a certain composer they are looking for other sensations.'

Soon, Prokofiev once again became the pianist on tour. Berlin (January 1925); United States (end of 1925); a tour of Italy ending in Naples, where the composer met Gorki (Spring 1926); a trip to Russia (1927); a series of a dozen symphony concerts and eleven concerts of chamber music in the United States followed by a tour of Canada and Cuba (1930) and, in addition, frequent recitals in all the European capitals.

In spite of his remarkable piano technique, Prokofiev held himself to long hours of study at the keyboard, dreaming, as he played over twenty or thirty times the same passage, of the symphonies and concertos which were not being written. But Prokofiev made demands on himself. He knew the price of perfection. Never would he allow the slightest negligence. This rigorous method is revealed in the following anecdote, recounted by the Soviet composer Kabalevsky:

'In 1937, when I was staying at the Hôtel de l'Europe in Leningrad, I heard one day the familiar sound of a piano in the neighbouring apartment. I did not think of it right away, but after a while I recognised some passages from the *Piano Concerto No. 3* of Prokofiev. They were being played so slowly, and certain isolated fragments were

95

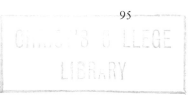

being repeated so many times and with such persistence, that it was not at first easy to recognise the work. This determined application to parts of the work continued all next day. Finally, on the third day, as I was coming back to my apartment, I met Prokofiev in the lift; my neighbour was none other than he. I lost no time in enquiring why he was practising so studiously a work he had for years been playing with remarkable ease on all the concert platforms of the world. Prokofiev replied: "The *Concerto No. 3* does not compare with the *Fifth*, which no-one ever plays and which is not known; everyone knows the *Third*—that is why I must know it perfectly." The next day, a concert of the work of Prokofiev took place in the Philharmonic Hall, where he played the *Concerto No. 3*, remarkably, as always.'[1]

From the moment of his arrival in Paris, and in spite of his apparent disinterest in modern Western music, Prokofiev seems to have flirted with polytonality and violently dissonant harmonies. In 1924, these new tendencies and this fleeting temptation towards modernism, were revealed in the *Symphony No. 2* and in the *Quintet Opus 39*. The precise influences are difficult to trace, but at least one can quote Stravinsky (the Stravinsky of the Octet), Ravel and perhaps even Roussel and Schoenberg.

With the *Symphony No. 2*, which belongs in the tradition of the *Sacre du Printemps* and the *Scythian Suite*, Prokofiev wanted to create a huge work of 'iron and steel' of which the general plan would recall the *Opus 111* of Beethoven. *The Symphony No. 2* consists of two movements: a *Sonata Allegro*, terribly aggressive and characterised by the most extraordinary drive; and a *Finale with variations*. Each of the six variations corresponds to a different atmosphere. The relationship between the orchestral sparkle of the fifth variation and the beginning of *Petrouchka* is distinctly noticeable.

The machine-like rhythms, the involved polytonal patterns, the noisy harmonies of the *Symphony No. 2* astounded earlier audiences, who were insensitive to the charm of this highly organised 'fierceness'. The unfavourable impression has unfortunately not yet been corrected, and critics of all opinions unite to condemn the work. According to Nestiev, the *Symphony No. 2* is 'an enormous edifice, complicated and loaded with sounds of which the frightful barbarism and terrible bellowings are not justified by any descriptive purpose . . .' and a French critic affirmed in February 1957, after the second Paris performance: 'In this Symphony, Prokofiev seems to have followed the advice of the poet Mayakovsky: "Let it make hay ! The Devil's own fodder !" ' In his autobiography, the composer himself made, as it were, an act of contrition: 'There was in it,' he says, 'a certain influence of the Parisian atmosphere where one feared

[1]The reminiscences of D. Kabalevsky (idem).

neither complications nor discords; and this was enhanced by my penchant for the working out of complicated themes.'

Noisy, perhaps, but 'complicated'? Beside the mildest of serial music, the *Symphony No. 2* of Prokofiev seems mere child's play.

Composed in the same spirit of quest, the *Quintet Opus 39*, despite the richness and originality of its instrumental fabric, did no more to convince the critics. Prokofiev undertook the composition of this work as the result of a commission from the 'Wandering Ballets' of Romanov, who wanted a ballet inspired by circus life under the title *Trapeze*. The *Quintet* is scored for oboe, clarinet, violin, viola and double bass and consists of six movements (the six episodes of the original ballet). Notwithstanding the sometimes polytonal scoring which is in fact totally alien to Prokofiev's genius, the melodic themes remain the essential support of the various parts; these themes, whether nostalgic or joyful, are of a markedly oriental character.

But the success of the work resides first and foremost in its variety, in the succession of lyrical passages and bounding rhythms, in the union of clearly defined motifs and complex harmonic patterns.

The first performance of the *Quintet* did not take place until 1927 in Moscow, and the work was then presented in Paris on 16th February, 1934, in the course of a concert organised by *Le Triton*.

The ensuing score marks the renewal of Prokofiev's relations with the Ballets Russes. After the performance of the *Symphony No. 2* in Paris in June 1925, Diaghilev, who had shown some coldness towards the composer as a result of a further brush between the friendly enemies, Prokofiev and Stravinsky, now proposed to the former to cement their collaboration with a new ballet on a Soviet subject. Diaghilev was probably thinking of the snobbism which would be agreeably titillated by a peep at the barbarians of the East, whereas Prokofiev, who had never broken off his ties with Russia, was enchanted with the offer. The plan for the *Pas d'Acier* (*The Steel Trot*) was rapidly sketched out with the aid of the painter-designer Georges Jacoulov:

'By comparison with the Quintet and the Symphony No. 2,' writes the composer, 'several changes are to be noted. The first was a move towards a Russian musical language, not that of the "Fairy Tales" of Afanassiev, but one which could describe contemporary life. The second a decisive step leading me towards chromatism and distonics. This ballet (for which Diaghilev had for some reason chosen

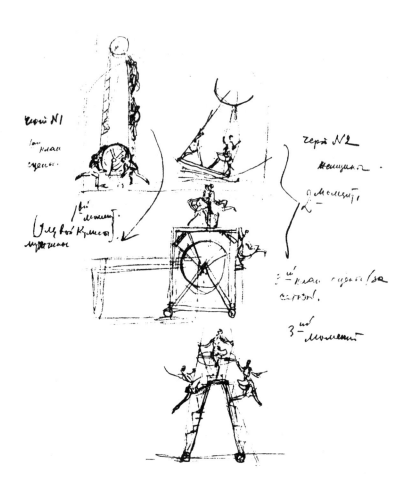

Sketch by Jacoulov for 'Le Pas d'Acier'

Tchernicheva, Lifar, Danilova and Massine in 'Le Pas d'Acier'

the title *Le Pas d'Acier*) is entirely constructed in some sort of diatonics and a whole series of themes is composed solely for white keys.'

The Steel Trot, of which the *Symphonic Suite Opus* 41 *bis* is particularly well known as a four-part excerpt,[1] is a skilful stylisation of scenes from Soviet life in 1920; the representation of factories with their vibrating roar and frenetic rhythms constitutes the most spectacular passage of a score at once colourful and light, fresh and at times witty.

Performed in Paris and in London in 1927 with choreography by Massine[2] *The Steel Trot* immediately aroused an armed insurrection against such 'bolshevik music', such 'mystification', such 'provocation'. Four years later, after the exportation of the ballet to the United States, Sarah D. Lowrie declared quite seriously in the *Evening Ledger* of Philadelphia that 'one wonders whether *The Steel Trot* is propaganda or music.'

As to 'bolshevik music', the voice of Soviet orthodoxy replies: 'Pro-

[1]Entrance of characters—Commissars, orators and citizens—The Sailor and the Factory Girl—The Factory.
[2]Creation in Paris at Théâtre Sarah Bernhardt, 7th June.

kofiev had never seen or known at first hand the Soviet reality . . . and the deeper meaning of the revolutionary movement signified for the creators of *The Steel Trot* nothing but a noisy, picturesque brawl, a mob of ranting, confused tub-thumpers, the rumble of a steam engine—all things which in no way differed from the mechanical subjects of urban art, so dear to the bourgeoisie. The vision of Soviet life was discredited in the eyes of the West, in spite of all the good will of the composer.'

However, the artist who hurled himself into 'cerebral and artificial' compositions and who 'discredited Soviet life' enjoyed a triumphant tour in Russia in 1927, the very year of the creation of *The Steel Trot*.

Certainly, since 1918, Prokofiev had become more of a traveller than an exile. He had never ceased to correspond with his friends, notably with Miaskovsky, whom he met in 1922 in Berlin. In May 1923 the journal *New Shores* published an article on Prokofiev, and some of his work was performed in Moscow and in Leningrad. Then on 18th February, 1926, on the stage of the Leningrad Opera, *The Love of Three Oranges* was produced, and was a success.

In January 1927 Prokofiev left Paris with his wife. What were his feelings on the eve of this decisive journey? A superfluous question, perhaps. Enthusiasm, intense happiness and emotion predominated over curiosity. Arriving in Moscow on 19th January, Prokofiev heard the *March* from the *Love of Three Oranges* played in his honour by the 'Persimfans'[1] Orchestra. He declared afterwards: 'You cannot imagine the intensity of my joy and pleasure.' During a period of three months, he was to give more than fifteen concerts in Moscow, Leningrad, Kharkov and Odessa and was greeted in every town and concert hall with quite exceptional enthusiasm.

The first programmes of symphonic music presented in Moscow and Leningrad included the *Suite* from the *Buffoon*, the *Piano Concerto No. 3*, the *Suite* from *The Love of Three Oranges*, the *Piano Concerto No. 2* and the *American Overture Opus* 42. This last work had been recently composed for the inaugural ceremony of the Aeolian Company Building in New York. Resolutely tonal, the *American Overture* has an extraordinary orchestration: two pianos; two harps; céleste; flute; oboe; two clarinets; bassoon; two trumpets; trombone; 'cello; two double basses and percussion—seventeen instrumentalists in all. The score, written for the occasion, is somewhat uneven and decidedly not one of its author's most inspired creations.

Certainly it disappointed the Soviet public, and afterwards there was, according to Prokofiev: 'a bewildered reaction, for the Overture had not got through to them.'

Symphony concerts were followed by piano recitals, and then came the first Russian performance of the *Quintet*. Every appearance evoked fresh manifestations of enthusiasm. The critics were warm. Assafiev wrote in the Leningrad *Red Gazette*:

[1]'Persimfans'—an orchestra without a conductor.

'The "Persimfans" Orchestra gave on 24th January a programme of works by Prokofiev with the composer also performing. The huge hall of the Conservatoire was full. There was an unusual attentiveness to be felt as the concert began—a feeling of expectancy and impatience and a certain air of festivity. . . . The arrival of Prokofiev was greeted by a fanfare and prolonged applause. After the execution of the *Piano Concerto No. 3* the happy mood which had at first prevailed intensified and was transformed into unanimous enthusiasm. . . . Prokofiev, as a composer and as a performer, is strong and powerful, clearcut and exuberant. In him are to be found just the qualities which are missing from our musical life today, despite its virtues. The triumphant reception accorded him by Moscow shows clearly that his artistic temperament is still nourished by an everlively creative energy, inspired by the country of his birth.'

It is interesting to note that Prokofiev *already* possessed 'just those qualities which are missing' from Russian musical life. So even before his return to the U.S.S.R. his aesthetic sense was in accordance with the broad lines of Soviet orthodoxy; the primacy of melody; simplicity of rhythms and harmonies; the affirmation of tonality, as well as those elements natural to his genius and which allowed him to reconcile without too much difficulty the demands of the régime with his creative personality.

During the course of this first visit, Prokofiev meets the young musicians of his country, expresses his admiration of a recent *Sonata* by Shostakovitch and of a *Septet* by Popov. At Odessa he encounters David Oistrakh, who has this to say about the Prokofiev concert:

'In March 1927 the composer himself arrived at Odessa, where he gave two concerts of his work at the Opera. It was a great event. Long before the concert began, the hall was full. All the musicians, music-lovers and young people had come to hear him and his success was tremendous. I do not know why, but a sort of festive atmosphere seemed to prevail. Never before had I felt so strongly impressed; and not by the music, which I knew very well already, but by its interpretation. I found Prokofiev's playing striking in its simplicity. Not a superfluous gesture, not a single excessive demonstration of feeling, nothing which could be interpreted as a desire to impress. By his way of presenting his work the composer seemed to be saying: "I do not want to 'embellish' my music—take it or leave it as it really is." One felt all the time as it were the purity of deep feelings. It was all unforgettable.'

After his return to Paris, the question in everyone's mind was: would Prokofiev make immediate plans for taking up permanent residence in Russia in the near future? His silence and impenetrability, of which his

Paris friends took due note, left the question open to speculation. There is, however, no doubt that Prokofiev had been deeply touched by the warm welcome his country had extended to him; he already knew that he was probably the most important of the Soviet composers and that, there, no Stravinsky could take his place. His old friends and the younger artists had made much of the material facilities which the régime offered to musicians, in particular the charm of the Composers' Union Hall which was placed at their disposal. After all, let it not be forgotten that official authority had not yet condemned, in 1927, works which did not conform to the Soviet realist dogma.

And so Prokofiev, who was to live another six years in Paris, had glimpsed the new Russia and at the same time rediscovered his mother country. His journey coincided with the composition of *The Steel Trot*, which marks his abandonment of the ephemeral modernistic tendencies expressed in the *Symphony No. 2* and in the *Quintet*.

Russian audiences, on their side, discovered the Western creations of Prokofiev. *The Love of Three Oranges* was mounted in Moscow whilst *The Gambler* and the *Symphony No. 2* were performed in Leningrad. All the same, one should not attach too much importance to the first fruits of his return to Russia. Prokofiev did not by any means 'renew' relations with the Soviets, since he had never broken them off. There is no 'turning-point' in Prokofiev's life, nor is there a 'break' in his artistic development. Only musicologists animated chiefly by pro- or anti-Soviet feeling have spot-lighted the composer's 'reversion'. But this reversion exists only in their slanted vision. The real drama concerns an 'uprooted' man, passionately in love with his country who, for *professional* reasons, had just made a journey abroad lasting fifteen years, and who had for a long time dreamed of his inevitable and final return to the Soviet Union.

Prokofiev still had the sound of his Russian success in his ears when, back in Paris, he took up the manuscript of *The Flaming Angel*, the orchestration of which was almost finished. The opera *The Flaming Angel*, for which Prokofiev had himself compiled a libretto after a story by Valerie Brioussov published in 1907, represents the 'opposite' of the *Love of Three Oranges*. A subject equally unreal leads us here into a dark intrigue where the sorcerers and magicians of the operetta have become the disquieting characters of mediaeval witchcraft. One no longer smiles at the spell cast by a bad fairy; one trembles at the delirious ravings of Renata the possessed.

The action takes place in the Rhineland of Germany in the sixteenth century. It is a Germany where new scientific discoveries vie with mediaeval superstition. The Knight Ruprecht, returning from an expedition to America, stops at an inn to spend the night there. Suddenly, he is awakened from his sleep by cries from the adjoining room. He gets up and, going into the room, he discovers a woman—Renata—in a state of profound exaltation, struggling with a vision. The young woman tells her story: when she was eight years old, a flaming angel appeared to her and became involved in her life, subjecting her to his will. But at sixteen, when she asked the angel to marry her, he replied in his fury that she must rediscover him in mortal form.

Renata believed she had recognised the flaming angel in the features of a certain Count Henri, who consented to live with her for a while. Turned away eventually by the Count, she is condemned to seek him without rest. Ruprecht, touched by the story and aware of Renata's charms, agrees to help her. The first Act ends with the arrival of a fortune-teller, who becomes highly excited on seeing blood in the young woman's hand.

In Act Two, Renata and Ruprecht, having left for Cologne, are plunged into the mysteries of sorcery and magical formulae. In the following Act, they find the house of the Count Henri, but the Count repulses the young woman with insults. Ruprecht challenges the Count to a duel. He is hurt and falls a prey to delirium. During the fourth Act Renata, in a hostelry in Cologne, announces to the Knight that she wishes to retire into a convent in order to expiate her sins. Ruprecht, in desperation, decides to kill himself. At this moment, Faust and Mephistopheles burst into the inn, engage in a series of escapades and finally invite Ruprecht to go with them. In the last Act, Renata has entered the Convent but has been tormented by demons ever since her arrival. The Grand Inquisitor exorcises them. She swears she has never had dealings with the Devil. But the nuns are then seized with an hysterical madness. In the presence of Mephistopheles, Faust and Ruprecht, the Grand Inquisitor condemns Renata to the stake.

The figure of Renata obviously dominates the action. She is a strange character, personifying the struggle of Good against Evil, for Renata is first and foremost a pure being, a creature who believes in the goodness of her flaming angel. But she is driven towards Evil, possessed by demons and by the Devil, who seems to be represented here by the Count Henri—a silent part in the opera—whose invisible presence plays a principal part throughout. The character of Ruprecht, although minutely drawn, takes second place. He is the *man*, any man, accidentally involved in a drama of sorcery. Then there is the 'clown' element introduced by the intervention of Faust and Mephisto; this is obviously farcical, since Prokofiev has curiously scored the part of Mephisto for tenor and that of Faust for baritone.

The subject of the opera demands a dramatic musical expression which the composer powerfully achieves: the 'chopped' Recitative of Renata in the first Act when she cries: 'Leave me! I beg you! Be gone!' accompanied by the breathless punctuation of the orchestra, or again the slow progression of the fortune-teller scene, achieve a rare expressive intensity. More than ever, Prokofiev has demonstrated in this score his enormous skill in instrumentation. The orchestral richness and the way in which the prosody treats the voice as an instrument pose delicate problems of execution, as the singers run the serious risk of being drowned by the accompaniment. The other difficulty resides in the length of the crushing rôle of Renata, who remains on stage for eighty-six minutes (the opera lasts nearly two hours).

The Flaming Angel is the fruit of a long maturing process. For eight years, an exceptionally long time for Prokofiev, the composer worked at the libretto and the orchestral score. During that time, he even felt the necessity to become acquainted with the locale of the piece and, probably for this reason, installed himself for eighteen months at Ettal.

In 1927, The Flaming Angel was completed. But the production did not take place until 1955 in Venice, under the direction of Nino San-zogno with Dorothy Dow in the part of Renata. Previously Bruno Walter had abandoned plans for a presentation at the Stadtische Oper in Berlin (1926) and, on 14th June, 1928, Koussevitsky had conducted the second Act of the opera in the Salle Pleyel. Among the cast were Nina Kochitz, the tenor Raïssof and the baritone Braminoff. In 1953, a concert performance of The Flaming Angel was given by Radiodiffusion Française and in November 1964 it took its place in the repertoire of the Opéra-comique.

The Flaming Angel has its Symphony. In fact, the themes of the opera had originally been composed for a symphonic score and, after finishing The Flaming Angel, Prokofiev picked out a part of the thematic material for the creation of the Symphony No. 3. This material thus returned to its original destination, stressed Prokofiev, adding: 'It seems to me that in this symphony I have managed to deepen my musical language. I should not like Soviet audiences to judge me by the March from the Three Oranges or by the Gavotte from the Classical Symphony.'

Indeed, after the formal elegance of the Classical Symphony and the discords of the Symphony No. 2, the Symphony No. 3 attains to a dramatic depth which relates it to The Flaming Angel even apart from the identity of certain themes. Of all his Parisian work, only the Symphony No. 3, which is innocent of all philosophical intention, and The Flaming Angel are possessed of such afflatus and intensity, and this despite a simplicity in the instrumentation unusual in the composer of the Scythian Suite and They are Seven. With its powerful lyricism, the Symphony No. 3 is truly a romantic symphony and if it were not for its somewhat elaborate harmony, one might say that it gives a presentiment of the symphonies of the Soviet period.

There is a remarkable unity of style in its four movements. The initial Moderato is constructed on two themes which, in the Flaming Angel, characterise the love and despair of Renata; the Andante corresponds to the beginning of the fifth Act of the opera, that is, to Renata's convent scene. For the third movement, the composer drew on the Finale of Chopin's Funeral Sonata: 'To begin with,' he says, 'there is a sort of perpetuum mobile on the strings; this owes something to the Finale of the Sonata in B flat minor of Chopin. The trio could be a canzonetta for several voices. Then the perpetuum mobile is taken up again, but this time fragments of the canzonetta themes are interspersed in it.'

An *Andante* which borrows certain parts of the theme of the first movement concludes the score.

The *Symphony No. 3*, completed on 3rd November, 1928, and dedicated to Miaskovsky[1] was first performed in Paris at the Salle Pleyel on 17th May, 1929, under the direction of Pierre Monteux. Public and critical reception was very favourable. Henry Malherbe wrote in *Le Temps*:

'. . . the rhythm and superposition of counterpoint suffice to create the musical climate. No striving after strange effects. A generous plan with well-defined contours. The orchestration, like the music itself, is hewn with great hatchet strokes. This close-knit work, intense and bold, was greeted with prolonged applause.'

On 21st May, 1929, four days after the first performance of the *Symphony No. 3*, the ballet *The Prodigal Son* scored a triumphant success at the Théâtre Sarah Bernhardt, thanks to the direction of Prokofiev, to the 'acrobatic' choreography of Balanchine, to the talent of Sergei Lifar, to the 'murky waterfront' décor of Rouault (his first scenic design) and thanks, finally, to the spareness and gravity of style of the score which, yet again, evidenced the diversity of Prokofiev's genius. The critic of *Le Temps* recognised that Prokofiev, the complex, involved, powerful, multiform artist, had in a way become emancipated.

It should perhaps be pointed out that this 'emancipation' really indicates a rapprochement to Western aesthetic values. Certainly *The Prodigal Son* does not proceed from the same mood as the *Quintet*, but the argument, drawn from the fifteenth Chapter of the Gospel according to Saint Luke, responds to a certain infatuation with antique subjects (this is the period of *Oedipus Rex* and the *Symphonie Psaumes*). Purity of expression and conciseness of instrumentation was also one of the aesthetic principles of this period. But the spareness of the *Prodigal Son* does not preclude lyricism, a lyricism which heralds *Romeo and Juliet*, nor does it preclude violence, as the composer uses it to describe the drunken scene.

'The idea of this ballet,' Prokofiev was to write later, 'was given me by Sergei Diaghilev in the autumn of 1928. When he put it to me, he was anticipating my desire to turn external effects towards interior lyricism. I devoted myself passionately to the composition and, before the New Year, a great part of the outline was accomplished. Diaghilev followed my work closely and often contributed interesting advice.

[1]Miaskovsky realised a piano transcription for four hands from the *Symphony No. 3*.

Drop curtain by Rouault for 'The Prodigal Son'

He attached special importance to the last scene and, when I telephoned him to say it was finished, he exclaimed: "What agony!" meaning to say that if the scene had not come off the whole ballet would be compromised. He came to hear it immediately and remained happy about it.'

Diaghilev's satisfaction was justified. The performance was one of the great successes of the Ballets Russes, but it was also the last, for Diaghilev, after having presented *The Prodigal Son* in Berlin and in London, died in Venice the following summer. This impresario-genius, who had attempted to arbitrate in the Stravinsky-Prokofiev duel, had brought to an end his association with the author of *Chout*, but the duel was not over.

The Prodigal Son, like *The Flaming Angel*, also has *its* symphony. But here the way Prokofiev went to work was different. He used thematic material from the ballet for three new scores: a *Symphonic Suite* in five parts, Opus 46 bis; *Six Piano Pieces*, Opus 52, one of which is the remarkable *Study* dedicated to Vladimir Horowitz; and then the *Symphony No. 4*.

Venice, 1925

The Symphony No. 4 provides 'important evidence of what I believe to be the truth', declared Henri Sauguet after the first French performance. 'This work is remarkable for its modesty. I mean that the composer has allowed the very lovely music to express itself quite naturally, without constraint, without any external strivings after colour, picturesque motifs, scholarly developments—in fact without any regard for any kind of modernism or aestheticism.'[1]

[1]*Europe Nouvelle.* 28th December, 1930.

Indeed, there are no constraints in this work. It was commissioned by the Boston Symphony Orchestra for its fiftieth anniversary and its success would seem to be the fruit of pure chance, since Prokofiev attached hardly any importance to the Symphony. It had been composed rapidly, with material from *The Prodigal Son* not used for the *Suite*, simply in order to satisfy the requirements of the Boston Symphony Orchestra. The first performance of the *Symphony No. 4* was directed by Sergei Koussevitsky in Boston on 14th November, 1930.

Then comes a new American commission: the *String Quartet No. 1*, strongly influenced by the Beethoven quartets, composed for the Library of Congress in Washington.[1] Ten years too late, the United States had discovered that the Titan pianist was also a composer.

Later, in 1930, the Théâtre National de l'Opéra took the same course as America and in its turn commissioned a work by Prokofiev. The result was disappointing and the ballet *On the Borysthenes*,[2] despite its picturesque Ukranian setting, was badly received. The critic René Dumesnil acknowledged, however, that 'the music was not alone responsible for this let-down. The choreography, arranged in the absence of the composer, altered the movements, and the décor and bizarre production confirmed the loosely woven nature of the score which, in the form of an orchestral suite, took its revenge'. A just revenge, for the work was dedicated to Sergei Diaghilev.

During the last years of the Western period, Prokofiev composed score after score. These works are either transcriptions (*Divertissement Opus 43*; *Sinfonietta Opus 48*; *Four Portraits from the Gambler Opus 49*) or pieces of lesser interest (*Things in Themselves*; *Two Sonatinas Opus 54*; *Three Pieces Opus 59*; *Sonata for Two Violins Opus 56*) and finally three concertos which merit closer examination.

The mystery which surrounded the fate of the *Piano Concerto No. 4* for so many years has now been solved.

In 1931 Prokofiev wrote a *Concerto for Left Hand* at the request of the Austrian pianist Paul Wittgenstein who had lost his right arm during the war. (It was Wittgenstein's disability that also prompted Ravel to write his famous *Concerto in D Major* and Richard Strauss to produce a *Parergon to the Sinfonia Domestica* and a *Panathenaenzug*, both for a left-handed piano and orchestra.) When he received the score, Wittgenstein's ungracious response was: 'Thank you for the Concerto, but I do not understand a single note and shall not play it.' However, he kept the score.

---

[1]The last movement of the Quartet, the Andante, the peak of the score, was transcribed by Prokofiev into one symphonic movement: *Andante for strings Op 50 b*.
[2]The old Greek name for the Dnieper.

With his children Sviatoslav and Oleg, Summer 1930

For twenty-five years it was accepted that the only score of the Fourth Concerto was lost or at least hidden by its dedicatee and, since no-one knew the work, rumour had it that its loss wouldn't be greatly felt.

However, in 1956 it was discovered that a *Concerto for Left Hand*, signed by Prokofiev, was being played in Eastern Europe (by the pianist Siegfried Rapp, who had also lost an arm as a result of a war wound). This Concerto, brought from Russia, was first performed in France by Georges Bernand at the Festival of Besançon on 11th September 1959. It also turned out that Rudolf Serkin had played the Concerto in 1958 with the Philadelphia orchestra. It was then suggested that there might be two versions: the original in the U.S.A., where Wittgenstein had fled in 1938, and a second version which had come to light in the U.S.S.R. This theory was borne out by information gleaned from Poulenc who, listening to the Soviet version 'would never have recognised' the score that Sergei Prokofiev had shown him twenty years earlier. But this was totally unfounded. The truth is not only less colourful, but also exceedingly simple because we know today that there is only the one Fourth Concerto—which belongs to Paul Wittgenstein. However, Prokofiev did keep a copy of this score and for some unknown reason, it lay undisturbed in a drawer right up to the time of his death.

Did Prokofiev have doubts about the quality of this ill-balanced work whose finale is only a miniature repetition of the initial Vivace? Or perhaps he preferred to forget (or reject?) those last works composed in a climate of Western decadence?

Achievement is no assurance of success. Although Gustave Samazeuilh declared in 1932 that 'the *Concerto No. 5* will certainly retain the attention of virtuoso pianists no less than the No. 3' this new score, created on 31st October, 1932, in Berlin under the direction of Furtwangler, is still almost unknown. Its flashing outlines, cut into by short themes, its dynamism, its use of contrast, nevertheless offer temptation to the pianist with agile fingers. It is true that the *Piano Concerto No. 5* is not exactly a 'pianist's Concerto'. The orchestral score is broadly developed and Prokofiev had thought of giving the work the title of *Music for Piano and Orchestra*.

What were Prokofiev's precise intentions?

'My essential problem in this Concerto,' he said in an interview he gave to the *Boston Evening Transcipt*, was to create a technique which would be different from that of my previous Concertos . . . an artist must always look for new modes of expression.'

The first three movements of the Concerto seem to be in absolute contradiction to this assertion. Certainly, the thematic element asserts itself less here than in previous Concertos, as the themes are more numerous and their development more closely knit. But each bar remains faithful to the original language of Sergei Prokofiev. The unusual division of the Concerto into five movements can nevertheless be noticed and in the two last of these there is a certain novelty. The large, lyrical cadence of the *Larghetto*, and the striving after sonority in the *Vivo*. But the *Piano Concerto No. 5* really belongs logically among the piano works of the composer.

It seems that the 'new mode of expression' suggested by Prokofiev is more applicable to the last Concerto of the Paris period, which was also to be the last orchestral score composed before the return to the U.S.S.R., namely the *Concerto for 'Cello and Orchestra Opus 58*.

Here, the composer, who employs all the resources of the 'Cello with incredible mastery, resumes some of the methods borrowed from

con forza

Western composers: rhythmic stylisation, elaborate chromatism, etc. But daring, with Prokofiev, never precludes melodic clarity and these two elements are to be found here right from the opening bars of the first movement.

Western audiences, to whom polytonality, atonality or dodecaphony are familiar, were hardly startled by the 'complex' scoring of the 'Cello Concerto; on the other hand, Soviet audiences, who were not so used to such ideas, rejected the work 'out of hand' (Nestiev); this set-back resulted in the composition by Prokofiev between 1950 and 1952 of a new 'Cello Concerto entitled Symphonie concertante pour violoncelle for the benefit of his compatriots.

The structure of the two works is similar, but whereas the three movements of the Concerto are of unequal length (the first being the shortest, the last the longest) the Symphonie concertante is divided into three parts of almost identical length. More particularly, the orchestration of the Symphonie concertante is less aggressive and the 'Cello part purer. The strange passion and restless lyricism of the Concerto have become appreciably 'healthier'.

Despite the subversive spirit of its bold conception, the 'Cello Concerto was already, chronologically, practically a Soviet work. Begun in 1933, it was finished in Russia and created in Moscow in 1938. In 1933 Prokofiev had abandoned the charms of Parisian life. In 1938 the break was complete. For a few years, the composer appeared from time to time in the West for tours and concerts, in the same way as from 1927 to 1933 he had made several visits to Russia for the tours of 1929 and 1932.

But it was worth noting that before leaving Paris Prokofiev at last seemed to have taken an interest in his French colleagues and took part in the activities of a new musical movement (Le Triton) alongside Henry Barraud, Jean Rivier, P-O. Ferroud and Marcel Mihalovici. It even seems that he attended meetings of the group with remarkable assiduousness. For the first concert of The Triton on 16th December, 1932 Prokofiev composed the Sonata for Two Violins Opus 56. On that same 16th December, the ballet On the Borysthenes was created at the Opéra and, next day, Prokofiev left for the United States on the last tour of his Western period.

The final return to Russia was at length decided upon. The composer had already agreed to write the music for a Soviet film: Lieutenant Kizhe. The tall, blond young man was still to be seen in the concert halls of the West. On 15th February, 1935, he gave a recital at Bologna, on 9th February, 1936, he performed at the Concerts Pasdeloup his Piano Concerto No. 3 and later conducted the first performance of his Egyptian Night suite. In January and February 1937 he played successively in Paris, Prague, Lausanne, Brussels, Bordeaux, Chicago, Saint-Louis and Boston. But in 1937 Russia demanded his contribution to the brilliant celebrations which were to mark the centenary of Pushkin's death. The com-

poser hastened to complete three symphonic scores: *Eugene Onegin*; *Boris Godounov* and *The Queen of Spades*. This Pushkin memorial heralded the end of his long travels. For Prokofiev, the Iron Curtain fell once and for all after a last tour of America in February 1938. Prokofiev had become the greatest Soviet composer. The title was supposed to be sufficient.

Five years earlier, the moment he arrived on his native soil, Prokofiev had demonstrated that he understood the task awaiting him. He had immediately declared in *Soviet Music*: 'When one comes back to the U.S.S.R. from abroad, one has the feeling of something quite different. Here, there exists a need for theatrical creation and there can be no doubt as to the kind of subject which is to inspire it: it must be heroic and constructive, for these are the attributes which most clearly characterise the present time.'

Prokofiev at work

P R K F

Extract from Larionov's sketch-book for the ballet 'Chout'

PRKF

'It is impossible to classify the personality of Sergei Prokofiev', declared the Italian composer, Gian Francesco Malipiero, recently, 'for he is neither the leader of a school, nor an innovator. It must surely be a difficult job for any critic to attempt to analyse him, or place him in any way in a period or a movement.'

It is true that Prokofiev does not fall easily into a definite category, that he has eluded fashions, systems, schools, movements and persuasions. He is not the leader of a school, despite the fact that he is now enjoying a following in Eastern Europe. He is not an innovator and yet his form of musical expression, consistently new, could not be exactly fitted to any previous method or formula.

In order to understand the work of Prokofiev, it would be as well to try to understand the man, to sketch a portrait, as it were.

Physically, according to Kabalevsky, 'he had a rather unusual profile, of the "sporting man" type, elegant clothes, a gay and benevolent expression like that of a young man.'

But this young man was not always benevolent. Generally silent ('he could keep quiet in three or four languages', as José Bruyr remarked) he would at times give way to temper which was no less violent for being cold. Certain remarks of his bordering on the uncouth have remained famous. What excuses had this violent man to offer? His absolute frankness, his intellectual honesty and, not least, the rigid discipline he applied to his own person. No complacency, which might have impeded the

Drawing of Prokofiev by Matisse, 1921

creation of the 'oeuvre Prokofiev', was permissible. The centre of the universe, the sole concern, the single objective was the composition of a work in which Prokofiev passionately believed.

As early as 1902 Gliere had summed up his pupil with the utmost accuracy. He insisted on Sergei's 'very strong character' as well as 'a will to work and a deep self-respect which manifest themselves especially in his professional activities'.[1]

All the evidence points to the love of work and the will to create which were Prokofiev's main characteristics. Madame Mendelssohn-Prokofiev, the second wife of the composer, has recorded:

'Sergei would not and could not imagine a single day without work ... He was capable of composing without table or piano, in a railway-carriage, a ship's cabin or a hospital. He would work no matter what

[1]The reminiscences of Gliere (idem).

mood he was in, in moments of euphoria or when he was in the doldrums . . . Being very strong-willed, he found it easy to do without many of the joys of life for the sake of the one he considered supreme: the joy of creation. Even before his illness, Sergei would refer to a day without work as "an empty, joyless day". In those days he would find it more and more difficult to tolerate any rest from his work, and when one asked how he was he would answer bitterly: "I'm vegetating".[1]

The composer, Dimitri Shostakovitch wrote of Prokofiev in his reminiscences: '. . . he would compose every day, even when doctors ordered him to rest. It was impossible for him not to do so, and those days when he was forced to "rest" were for him the most painful ones. . .'[2]

In the circumstances, it is not surprising that the composer, who died at the age of 62, should have managed, in spite of an arduous career as a pianist and occasionally as a conductor, to produce 131 works at a time when prolific output of the Mozart or Vivaldi type was becoming more and more rare.

Prokofiev's daily work was, moreover, strictly regulated. 'Sergei would generally compose in the morning', Madame Mendelssohn-Prokofiev tells us 'until one or two o'clock in the afternoon. He always got up early, and it was chiefly during the morning hours that he wrote the main part of his work. Whilst he was composing, one had not to ask him anything. He would be so absorbed by his thoughts, so intent, that he would react very nervously to any outside interruption. Between five and eight o'clock in the evening, Sergei would start work again, but it would be inaccurate to count as working hours only those he spent at the piano or the work table. Whatever he was doing, he would always come back to music.'

In fact, Prokofiev was what is commonly called a devil for work. He did not pile opus on opus for the purpose of delivering an eternal message to the world—passionately as he believed in his achievement as a musician and in his present and future fame—but he could not conceive of life without work, daily work, and the artist was not excluded from this general law. He would have made a dedicated engineer or a conscientious doctor. He would have followed any calling with the same seriousness, the same love of work well done. He was simply an inspired artisan.

In no way tormented by intellectual speculation outside music, (although he became involved, during his Paris period, with the Christian

---

[1] The reminiscences of Mme. Mendelssohn-Prokofiev (idem). The very young poet Mira Mendelssohn, having been the composer's collaborator, became his wife in about 1940. Prokofiev had left his former wife in particularly painful circumstances, together with his two children, who still live in the U.S.S.R.
[2] The reminiscences of Dimitri Shostakovitch (idem).

МОСОБЛАСТКОМРАБИС

КЛУБ МАСТЕРОВ ИСКУССТВ

9 НОЯБРЯ

ШАХМАТНЫЙ МАТЧ
ДАВИД   СЕРГЕЙ
ОЙСТРАХ-ПРОКОФЬЕВ
УСЛОВИЯ МАТЧА:

Открытие матча 9 ноября 1937 года в 9 часов вечера

Poster announcing a chess match between Oistrakh and Prokofiev

Science Movement) and indifferent to the fundamental musical evolution of our time which led the famous *Tristan* chord along the road to *Pierrot Lunaire* and the *Marteau sans Maître*, he was a man who worked and an artist who created with passionate sincerity, but with immense pride as well, and with complete consciousness of the originality of his genius.

How did Prokofiev approach the other problems of life? He seems to have been in all circumstances the rigorously methodical man described by Madame Mendelssohn-Prokofiev. He loved figures and the exact sciences.

'All the new things in life: science, techniques, art, attracted Prokofiev. He would look on a map for the place where a new power station was being built, or a railway line, or a canal and would watch with absorption an agricultural machine working in a field . . .'

His love of precision is also revealed in a curious kind of writing where the vowels are often omitted, so that, for instance, Prokofiev becomes PRKF.

The choice of pastimes and relaxations rounds off the portrait perfectly. Very much the gambler, Prokofiev loved bridge and adored chess, which he had played in masterly fashion since the age of seven.

One has to submit to the evidence: despite the lyricism of, say, *Romeo and Juliet* and the tender irony of *The Love of Three Oranges*, Prokofiev was not a poet. He preferred mathematics to the plastic arts and when he buried himself in a book, it was to look for a new subject for an opera or oratorio. He placed Tolstoy above Dostoïevsky and, for the décor of his operas, he was just as pleased with the Larionov maquettes as with those of Picasso. He was hardly interested at all in museums or monuments and, when he first found himself confronted with a famous French cathedral, he meditated for a while and then said: 'I wonder how they managed to get the sculptures up there.' Motoring he found particularly exciting, but he was less of a gourmand for the beauties of nature and the treasures of art than for the gastronomic pleasures. Towards 1930, Prokofiev had decided to go with his wife and Nabokov on a 'gastronomic tour of France'. The tour was long and tiring, for 'a large part of the journey was spent ordering, eating and digesting meals.' Unfortunately, the pleasures of the table did not succeed in dissipating a certain tension in the marital atmosphere. When Lina wanted to visit a *château* or a cathedral, Prokofiev would go off in search of a 'three-star restaurant' and when his young wife would have liked a cosy inn where one could look out over some green valley, the composer would insist on following the Michelin Guide.

The journey entailed plenty of significant incident. For example, a halt at Domrémy, where Lina and Nabokov wanted to make a rather touching pilgrimage, let loose one of Prokofiev's frightful tempers. He had not 'provided for' this little detour and when the unhappy Lina hung about for a little while in the streets of Domrémy when it was time for them to go Prokofiev burst out: 'What does this behaviour mean? What do you take me for? I'm not your lackey to have to wait about for you like this. You can take your suitcase and get on the train.'

Prokofiev's face was 'blue with rage'. Lina burst into tears. A sad situation, brought about by a too punctillious character, obsessed with exactitude and precision.

According to Nabokov, Prokofiev was in the habit, during his stay in Paris, of making a daily tour of the Dôme des Invalides in accordance with a judiciously timed itinerary. He would do this as a sort of apéritif. One morning, Nabokov himself took part in this race against time.

'You know,' confided the composer, 'it's a sort of ritual with me. I started a year ago. I come out before lunch and walk up the Avenue de Breteuil. Then I turn right at the end and then left, and when I get to the front of the Invalides, I am beginning to feel hungry. After that, I can think of nothing but food. I'm ready to swallow five luncheons. You'll see. In a little while you'll be feeling the same . . .'

The exercise is rigorously planned, down to the smallest detail. 'It

Depression is a lie of the mortal mind, consequently it cannot have power over me, for I am the expression of Life, i.e. of divine activity:

1. I am the expression of Life, i.e. of divine activity

2. I am the expression of spirit which gives me power to resist all what is unlike spirit.

3. My fidelity grants my uninterrupted adherence to all what is true.

4. I am the expression of Love which sustains my constant interest in my work.

5. My individuality is given me to express beauty.

6. As I am the expression of Mind, I am capable of vigorous creative thinking.

7. As I am the effect of the one great Cause, I ignore everything which does not proceed from this Cause.

8. I am the expression of joy, which is stronger than aught unlike it.

9. I am the expression of perfection, and this leads me to the perfect use of my time.

10. I am in possession of health, therefore I work with ease

11. I have wisdom in order to constantly express it.

12. I am the image of Mind; this keeps me busy to express inspired thoughts.

13. I am honest to myself and therefore will do the work which is the best.

14. As activity is my inherent quality, the desire to work is natural.

15. Whereas I am the expression of Soul, I feel the necessity to express beauty.

16. I am spiritual, consequently vigorous.
17. Infinite Life is the source of my vitality.
18. At every moment I am alert to express beautiful ought.
19. I am eager to work, as action is the expression of Life.
20. I rejoice in tribulations, for the contact with them gives a proof of their the opportunity to prove their unreality.
I am ——— The realities of Lt.

There is no m. m. t. express any disharmonious beliefs of material body.

. I am the thinking of immortal mind in evidence.

Extracts from Prokofiev's personal notebooks, found in Paris in 1959

takes me exactly 26 minutes 17 seconds to 26 minutes 35 seconds from door to door . . . I always arrive here, in front of this house, four minutes and 10 seconds after leaving my own doorstep . . .'

This completes, quite logically, the portrait of Prokofiev. It is the same man who has a passion for power stations, who wins chess tournaments and keeps an eye on his watch on solitary walks.

If, to take up Malipiero's theme again, the musicologist has a 'difficult job' with Prokofiev, matters would seem to be simpler for the psychologist. There is a disassociation between the artist and the man, between the musician expressing himself through his sensibilities and the amateur of exact science. It is well known that certain composers have found their way about equally well in poetry (Schumann) or in some other art form, as did Mozart or Schubert. But Prokofiev could only be a musician. His feelings are aroused—he becomes a poet—only when he is seated at the piano or browsing over instrumentation. The cold, distant, sarcastic and at times violent temperament could be misleading, as in certain aggressive passages from the early scores; but in many instances his sensibility is spontaneously expressed. In order to compose his *Violin Concertos*, the chess-player became, in spite of himself, a poet.

Prokofiev's hands

Prokofiev at a game of chess

The Return of the Prodigal

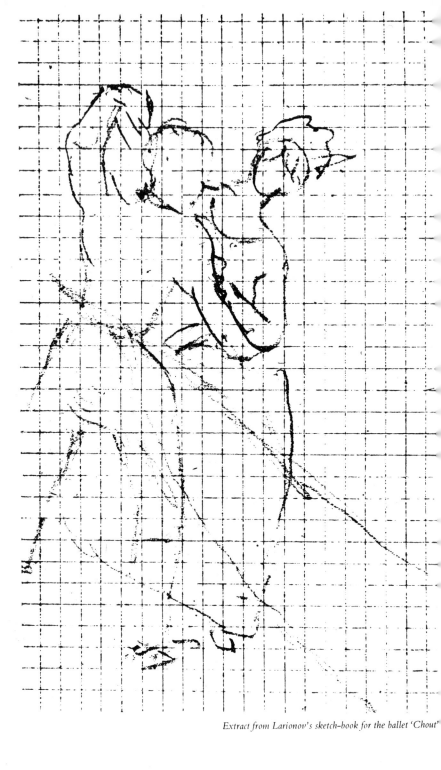

Extract from Larionov's sketch-book for the ballet 'Chout'

THE RETURN OF THE PRODIGAL

Aram Khatchaturian gave the following definition of the Soviet composer:

'In the Soviet Union, the composer occupies a place of honour. He benefits by the attention and sollicitude of the people. His material comfort is assured. He knows that his work is necessary and highly appreciated by Society. Moreover, he has, of course, a deep consciousness of his responsibility towards Society, towards history and towards humanity.'

Prokofiev was apparently willing to assume this responsibility when he returned to Russia. He made the sudden discovery of an unprecedented social revolution, enabling millions of men and women to flock into concert halls for the first time. In a number of articles, he developed his ideas on the subject of Soviet music, affirming:

'I would describe the music needed here as "light serious" or "serious light" music; it is by no means easy to find the term which suits it. Above all, it must be tuneful, simply and comprehensibly tuneful, and must not be repetitious or stamped with triviality.' (*Izvestia*, 16th November, 1934) and again:

'The time is past when music was composed for a circle of aesthetes. Now, the great mass of people in touch with serious music is expectant

In the studio of the sculptor Maniezer

and enquiring ... The search for a musical language which corresponds to socialist times is a difficult one, but it presents a noble problem for a composer. In our country, music has become the domaine of enormous masses of people. Their taste and their artistic desires are developing at an extraordinary rate. And the composer must "correct" every one of his new works in terms of this evolution ... This is why any attempt by a composer at simplification is an error. To endeavour to place himself within reach of the audience is a belittlement both of the maturity of its culture and of the evolution of its taste. Any such attempt carries an element of insincerity' (1937).

This idea of remaining accessible to the greatest number without condescending and without simplifying the means of artistic expression represents the whole ambiguity of Soviet music. In fact, as Rostislav Hofman showed, an avant-garde art, an art of the Left, is generally for a small number of the initiated. Politics of the Left, on the other hand, are those which have to depend on the vast mass of a population. So a 'reactionary' régime can adapt itself to an art of the Left, but a 'progressive' political line must tolerate only the most orthodox, the most social, the most popular there can be—in the best sense of the term.[1]

In the phase immediately after the October Revolution, indeed, all artistic excesses were allowed. Avant-garde art was in demand. Then, gradually, it appeared quite clearly that the creators were detaching themselves from the vast masses which the régime claimed to be serving, and they were made to conform. Prokofiev returned to Russia just precisely when the reaction against these modernist adventures was gaining the upper hand, and the Soviet authorities lost no time in identifying Prokofiev's art with their own musical conceptions.

In 1929, V. Meyerhold had declared over Moscow Radio: 'Prokofiev's lyricism is peculiarly shot through with a strong virility. It is not a world limited within itself. It is not the product of detachment from reality, nor of insubstantial dreaming. Prokofiev's lyricism is the outcome of his vital happiness; it is that of a man who has embraced life, and whose act of creation is taking place at the very heart of life, rejoicing in its problems ... It is remarkable that these essential features of Prokofiev were apparent from the start, when he came forward with his work in advance of our times, fighting for them against the sickly sweet, highly-spiced, over-refined music cultivated in the hot-houses of "aesthetic" modernism, struggling against all decadent tendencies. The *Scythian Suite* of 1915 could not fail to attract to itself the furious attack of the whole bourgeois coalition. It launched an attack on the philistines themselves ... Now, Prokofiev is at the height of his powers. Let us rejoice in his bold and courageous music, for it infuses the much-desired energy into us which is so necessary to us for our work.'

[1] R. Hoffmann, *Music in Russia*.

131

Although he may have been eminently suited to become the 'model Soviet composer', Prokofiev had to face new demands from 1933 onwards. On the practical level, how did he respond to the call of his country? What are to become the predominant features in his work?

One fact has been confirmed: Prokofiev was composing a greater and greater number of works. Whereas the twenty-six years between 1907 and 1933 produced fifty-nine works (*opus* 1 to *opus* 59); the Soviet period produced seventy-eight, but of these only fifty-eight were complete, autonomous works: four operas, five oratorios, three symphonies, three ballets, one concerto, one quartet, eight sonatas, and stage and film music.

The value of a work of art is never quantitative, of course, but nevertheless, this important accumulation of scores, of varying worth, once more proves the frenetic creative will of the composer, who was not only to refuse to give any more concerts after 1942, so as to be able to devote all his time to composition, but was to abandon even the publication of his autobiography.

It has already been asserted several times that there was no 'artistic break' in 1934. When Prokofiev became a Soviet composer, as author of the *Quintet* and the *Symphony No. 2*, he nevertheless abandoned the ephemeral influences of the West. He was looking for harmonic simplification and drew generously on his marvellous reserves of thematic material. He ended by casting aside violent orchestrations and more often gave full play to his lyricism. The simplification and purification of an art are also the mark of a creator who has passed through the difficult waters of youth, and it is possible that, independently of the political context, Prokofiev had undergone that evolution.

Nonetheless, certain concessions to the régime were inevitable, and in particular the choice of subjects for his operas:

'It is difficult to write an opera on a Soviet subject,' writes Prokofiev. 'The processes of classical opera would seem strange and useless to the new public, new sentiments and new customs to be found here. The subject undertaken must not be inert and petrified, nor, on the other hand, too educational. The characters must be well and truly alive, with passions, loves, hates, pleasures and sorrows flowing naturally from their new mode of life.'

There were certain works of 'homage' to be undertaken as well, such as the *Cantata for the 20th Anniversary of the October Revolution* on texts of Marx, Lenin and Stalin, scored for symphony orchestra, military orchestra and accordion and percussion band; and such as the *Toast to Stalin* on popular texts or the Cantata for the *30th Anniversary of the Revolution*. The musical value of these enormous canvases does not come into question for, like too many of the works of the period, they are not yet known in the West.

The first score composed after the return of Prokofiev to Russia was the music for the Feinzimmer film: *Lieutenant Kizhe*. This was the first time Prokofiev had worked for the cinema.

The subject of *Lieutenant Kizhe* is inspired by an administrative mistake which was perpetrated in the time of Tsar Paul I. The negligence of a bureaucrat in connection with an official, and thus sacrosanct, document, was artfully covered by the creation of a fictitious Lieutenant Kizhe (as the result of an untranslatable play on words). The idea rapidly took on that this Lieutenant Kizhe was a veritàble blessing in disguise. He could shoulder the responsibility for all the stupidities committed by faithful servants of the Tsar, until the day when the latter exiled him to Siberia to atone for his errors. In a sudden burst of clemency, however, the Tsar decided to recall Kizhe who, after a succession of promotions, reached the rank of General. When finally Paul I expressed the desire to make the acquaintance of this remarkable officer, he was informed that he had just died.

The five tableaux of the orchestral suite taken from the film music represent successively the birth of Kizhe, announced by a distant fanfare; a Romance, the story of the Lieutenant's love; the marriage of Kizhe to the accompaniment of a particularly comic, ponderous wedding march; then a long-drawn-out troika (this is Russia, after all) and, finally, the burial of Kizhe, a résumé of previous themes, ending with the echoes of a distant fanfare. The nice balance of stylisation and musical parody have largely contributed to the popularity of the suite.

The stage music for *Egyptian Nights* by Taïrov, although composed around the same time as *Lieutenant Kizhe*, is far less well-known. Nevertheless, the play, which was performed seventy-five times at the Kamerny Theatre in Moscow in 1935, has a certain originality, uniting as it does elements of Shakespeare's *Antony and Cleopatra* with Pushkin's *Egyptian Nights* and the *Caesar and Cleopatra* of Shaw. It was repeated in London and the incidental music, transformed into an orchestral suite, was first performed by the Concerts Pasdeloup in Paris on 9th February, 1936, under the direction of the composer.

The same year, Prokofiev wrote his *Violin Concerto No. 2* for the French violinist Robert Soetens. This Concerto, which was originally designed to take the form of a grand Sonata, was begun in Paris and finished in Voronezh and in Baku. The world première was given in Madrid on 1st December, 1935, by the Madrid Symphony Orchestra with Robert Soetens under the direction of Enrique Arbos and in the presence of the composer. Prokofiev then embarked on a mediterranean tour which took him to Spain and Portugal and then to North Africa. Two months later, Soetens created the Concerto before a Parisian audience and the critics were not mistaken: the *Violin Concerto No. 2* clearly belongs in the same line as the *Concerto in D Major* written

With Kontchalovsky and Sofronitzky, 1934

eighteen years earlier. There is the same lyricism, the same rich melodic line, the same variety of mood, the same balance between violin and orchestra. Did this mean that the inspired author of *Romeo and Juliet* was rejoining the stormy creator of the *Scythian Suite*? It did not, but when Prokofiev uses the same raw material, the same musical form (this time, the Violin Concerto) he rediscovers the same accents, for his genius has the same aspect in 1935 as in 1937.

Nevertheless, the lyricism of the *Concerto No. 2* is at the same time recaptured in a great ballet score composed on the theme of *Romeo and Juliet*.

At the time of the *Scythian Suite*, the critic Kolonitsev remarked

onically: 'Everyone does what he can. There are those who sing the
ove of *Romeo and Juliet*, others who are only good for imitating the
urious cries of monkeys and their disorderly frolics.' The response was
orthcoming, and conclusive: the road from *The Buffoon* and the *Scythian
Suite* was to end in a *Romeo and Juliet* in the best romantic tradition.

Prokofiev's ballet, commissioned by the Moscow Theatre, is conceived as a silent opera. Its length is unusual (it lasts two and a half hours)
and its conception very Shakespearian, seeking to project the true
psychology of the two protagonists. The score does, in fact, suffer from
certain 'longueurs' and even from some banality, but it has charm
nevertheless by reason of its contrasts of violence and tenderness and of
the great beauty of its themes.

Already in 1935 the theatrical producer Radlov had studied with
Prokofiev the staging of the ballet. But *Romeo* waited five years to be
presented to the Leningrad public, with the celebrated Galina Ulanova,
on 11th January, 1940. The ballet had been created two years previously
at Brno, in Czechoslovakia, and Sergei Lifar later mounted it (in 1955) at
the Paris Opéra, after having considerably pruned down the score.

A ballet lasting two and a half hours can obviously not be performed
very often. As was his custom, Prokofiev found a way round this obstacle
by composing three symphonic suites taken from *Romeo and Juliet*, the
first two in 1935 and the third ten years later. These suites felicitously
combine the lyricism, fire and humour of his earliest work. The lively,
sprightly *Danse populaire* of the first Suite is followed by a delicately
poetic *Madrigal*, a majestic *Minuet* with a touch of wit here and there, and
tender *Romeo and Juliet* which wonderfully expresses the dawning of
love. The other two Suites are in the same vein, dominated by a delicious
portrait of *Juliet* (second Suite) through which burst the vivacity and
freshness of youth, the deeply expressive song of *Romeo at the Tomb of
Juliet* and the broad lyrical quality of *Romeo at the Fountain*.

Having proved to the Soviet public that he was capable of singing the
love of *Romeo and Juliet*, Prokofiev wanted to turn his attention to the
children and, taking up again the mood of the *Ugly Duckling*, he composed the famous *Peter and the Wolf*, an entertainment and an educational
work designed to acquaint his young audience with the various orches-
tal instruments. There is no recipe for the success of a score for children.
Any musician will agree that it is a gamble. This one came off beyond all
expectations. Russian, French or American children alike tremble when
Peter boldly tackles the wolf. The great conductors of our time (Leh-
mann, Karajan) have directed the miaouwing of the cat-clarinet and the
warbling of the bird-flute.

Unfortunately, there will never be another *Peter and the Wolf*. Neither
Summer Day, nor the *Winter Bonfire* will redound to Prokofiev's credit.
But in the catalogue of children's fables, *Peter and the Wolf* has found a
place beside *Snow White* and *Tom Thumb*.

Is *Peter and the Wolf* only for children? Surely. But there are some wh[o] claim that the score might equally well be an 'oeuvre à clé', with politic[al] allusions. Here is Peter, the Soviet Man, brave and realistic. Then there [is] the bourgeois transformed into a duck who, in decisive moment[s] cautiously hides away in the marshes; then the socialists transformed int[o] huntsmen, noisily demonstrating their ineffectuality.

In 1936, the year of *Peter and the Wolf*, Prokofiev also composed thre[e] musical illustrations for the centenary of the death of Pushkin, music fo[r] the film *The Queen of Spades* and two theatrical scores for *Boris Godouno[v]* and *Eugene Onegin*. The three Pushkin scores, where the shades o[f] Moussorgsky and Tchaikovsky are to be found prowling dangerousl[y] around, have never been performed.

The *Cantata for the 20th Anniversary of the Revolution*, of the sam[e] period, did not have a public hearing until 1966, despite its five hundre[d] instruments and the precious time which its creation cost the compose[r] It was certainly not easy to put to music 'the speech made by Stalin ove[r] the tomb of Lenin' or 'the report of Stalin at the Eighth Extraordinar[y] Congress of Soviets', but 'in spite of their liveliness and wealth o[f] imagery, the speeches of the great figures of the Revolution are no[t] designed to be sung in chorus. In fact, when they are, the text loses on th[e] one hand its oratorical value and its strength of conviction, and on th[e] other it weighs down the melodic language' (Nestiev).

So, in 1936, there is only a single truly original score: *Peter and th[e] Wolf*. The years 1937 and 1938 seem to be even less fertile: only a fe[w] choruses and the incidental music for *Hamlet* were composed at this time A curious silence for a musician who could not let a day pass withou[t] working. Perhaps he was not fully conscious yet of his responsibilitie[s] towards the Soviet people, or was it that he was seeking a differen[t] direction? He had just been on a visit to the West and his old friend[s] found him peculiarly reserved about his new life; he was probably takin[g] his bearings before embarking on a new period of intense creative work

It would, moreover, be wrong not to accredit to the year 1938 th[e] beginnings of a major enterprise: the collaboration of Prokofiev an[d] Eisenstein. In May of that year, the film producer had already propose[d] to the composer that he should write a score for the film *Alexande[r] Nevsky*, thus enabling Prokofiev to find his way back to epic wor[k] which, since the *Scythian Suite* he had allowed to fall into oblivion.

Eisenstein, one of the greatest geniuses in the twentieth century worl[d] of art, whose culture and musical taste extended far beyond the limits o[f] the film, had conceived, for *Alexander Nevsky* an 'audio-visual' construc-tion, 'uniting', in the words of Jean Mitry, 'all the values and suggestiv[e] powers of music with all the values and suggestive powers of visual art organising them into a univocal whole to achieve a more complex, mor[e] total expression of the same ideas and emotions.'

The boldness of this notion of audio-visual counterpoint in the field o[f] the cinema can be judged from the fact that, twenty years after Eisenstei[n]

Eduard Tissé, Eisenstein and Prokofiev parodying 'Alexander Nevsky'

conceived the idea, the mine does not seem to have been worked again. The realisation of Eisenstein's concept necessitated a very close collaboration between the film maker and the composer. Prokofiev describes the artistic encounter as follows:

'When Eisenstein suggested to me that I should write a score for the film *Alexander Nevsky*, I accepted with pleasure, for I had for a long time admired his magnificent talent as a producer. In the course of our work interest never failed to grow and Eisenstein revealed himself not only as a brilliant producer but as a very fine musician. The action, placed in the thirteenth century, is built up on two opposing elements: on the one hand the Russians, on the other hand the Teuton Crusaders. The natural temptation was to use the music of the time, but the study of the catholic chants demonstrated that, over seven centuries, these had become so far removed from us and their emotional content had become so alien, that they no longer sufficed to feed the imagination of the spectator. This was why it was much more interesting to interpret them, not as they had been at the time of the Battle on the Ice, but as we should feel them today. Once the music was composed, its recording played an important part. In spite of enormous and continuous progress, the recording had not reached perfection—when the idea

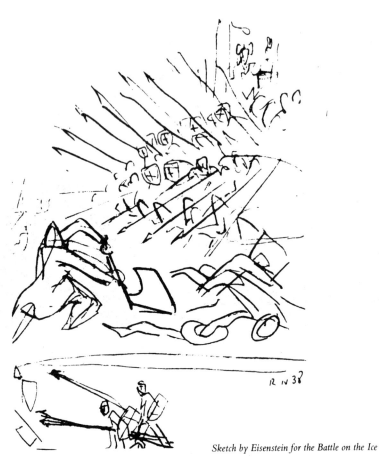

Sketch by Eisenstein for the Battle on the Ice

came to me to see whether it was possible to use the "negative" sides of the microphone in order to obtain particular effects. It is, of course, known that a violent blast of sound through the microphone will spoil the film and cause a disagreeable noise. As the sound of Teuton trumpets was without doubt disagreeable to Russian ears, I had the fanfares played straight into the microphone, which provoked a curious dramatic effect . . . The cinema is a young art, and like the present time, it offers new and interesting possibilities for the composer to exploit; he must deepen these possibilities and not content himself with writing music which he then passes on to the people in the studios responsible for synchronising it . . .'[1]

[1] *The Soviet historical film*, March 1940.

It is obvious that Prokofiev's researches were stimulated and rendered possible by the presence of a producer like Eisenstein, who had perfectly understood the genius of his collaborator: 'The music of Prokofiev', he wrote, 'is astonishingly plastic, never illustrative; it shows in an amazing way the inward progress of events, their dynamic structure in which emotion and the sense of what is happening take definite form.'

We know that *Alexander Nevsky*, that masterpiece of epic filming, depicts the invasion of Russia by the cruel Teutonic Knights, whose atrocities the spectator is not spared; thanks to the courage of *Alexander Nevsky*, the inhabitants of the region of Pskov regroup themselves and turn away the Knights in the course of the famous battle on the frozen Lake Tchoudsk. The battle scene constitutes practically half the film.

Every moment of the musical score responds to the demands of filmic expression. Thus Prokofiev, when describing the bareness of a Russian landscape, keeps his medium under strict control:

And yet Prokofiev's work was able to liberate itself magnificently from the context of the picture. In the form of a Cantata in seven parts, of which the highlight remains the famous Battle on the Ice, the film music has become one of the most imposing and dramatic of Soviet musical works.

So, *Alexander Nevsky* opens the period of the great Soviet compositions of Prokofiev. From 1939 onwards, they followed one another in varying forms at an ever-increasing rate: symphonies, chamber music, operatic works, every musical form inspires the composer, who now knows that the Soviet artist *must*, by his work, respond to the confidence of the régime which grants him a privileged position. Thanks to his faith in Communism, or thanks to his docility towards his new masters, Prokofiev 'can be considered as the ideal Soviet artist, the ideal of the great artist who has known how to live the same sort of life as the people of his country, to respond to their every movement, to think with them, rejoice with them and suffer with them'[1] (Shostakovitch).

To excite the patriotism of the Soviet people, Prokofiev composed *Simeon Kotko* and, to amuse them, *The Betrothal in the Monastery*. These two operas, the first operatic works after his return to Russia, are more or less contemporaneous. *Simeon Kotko*, inspired by a story of Kataïev: 'I am the son of the working people', retraces an episode from the Ukrainian revolt of 1918. Its historical and political intentions are praiseworthy and Prokofiev, to emphasise the power of its expression, tried to avoid static passages and choruses by mingling spoken words with singing and by using massed chorales for animated scenes.

'In composing my opera,' he says, 'I was concerned with theatrical movement so that the dramatic action should not slow down at any point.'

However, the first Moscow performance on 23rd June, 1940, provoked lively political controversy and 'the debate was not concluded until December, during the course of a conference attended by delegates from the various Republics of the Soviet Union' (Nestiev).

No such misadventure awaited *The Betrothal in a Monastery*, after Sheridan's *Duenna*. The choice of subject proves that Prokofiev does not wish to limit himself to dealing with heroic or educational problems. His intentions are revealed in his own words:

'When I began the opera about the Duennas,' he writes, 'I saw two possibilities: the first was to underline in the music the comic side of the work, the second to rely on the romantic aspect. I chose the second solution . . . The construction of the Sheridan play, which contains a number of songs, made it possible for me, without holding up the action, to write a whole series of small pieces, serenades, ariettas, duets, quartets and large ensembles. Numerous texts based on Sheridan were written by Mira Mendelssohn with whom I later made the libretto of *War and Peace*.'[2]

The first presentation of *The Betrothal*, fixed for 1941, was put off as a result of the German invasion. In 1943, new plans for a stage production at the Bolshoi Theatre in Moscow also fell through and the work was not shown in public until 30th November 1946 at Leningrad.

Variety in work, this was one of Prokofiev's favourite by-words and

[1] *The Symphony of Light and of the Joy of Living. Soviet Music* 1957.

[2] Written for the Sovinform Bureau, 26th March, 1943 (idem).

so, after finishing his two operas, he undertook several sonatas—a form he had practically abandoned during a period of about fifteen years. One after the other came three *Piano Sonatas*, a *Sonata for Violin and Piano*, then a *Flute Sonata*, the future *Second Violin Sonata*.

Was Prokofiev's Chamber Music influenced by Soviet ideas?

In the *Sonata for Violin and Piano No. 1 Opus* 80, sketched out in 1938 and accomplished eight years later, there is a freshness of inspiration, a lyricism and a thematic wealth in no way contradictory to the spirit of the two Violin Concertos. In this Sonata, Prokofiev 'was seeking a clear, melodious language without renouncing universally recognised melodic and harmonic arrangements. There lies the difficulty of composing clear music: it must be a new clarity.'

This melodic arrangement, which is not 'new' in Prokofiev, is associated with simple, well-defined rhythmic formulae which reappear throughout his work.

In 1943, Prokofiev composed a *Sonata for Flute and Piano*, as 'this instrument had for a long time attracted me and it seemed to me that it had been made little use of in musical literature. I wanted this Sonata to have a classical, clear, transparent sonority.'

In the same melodic vein as the *Violin Sonata No. 1*, it possesses, in addition, a humour and fantasy more in keeping with the lightness of a flute. At the request of the violinist David Oistrakh, and acting upon his advice, Prokofiev transcribed the Sonata for the violin the following year and slightly modified the flute part. In these two forms, Op. 94 and 94 bis, the Sonata represents one of the most charming achievements of the composer.

Three works composed between 1939 and 1944 also link up with the series of Piano Sonatas, and it is in these scores in fact that the continuity in Prokofiev's work is most clearly to be seen. It is obvious that the pianistic mastery of the *Suggestion diabolique* and the *Toccata Op.* 11 (1910-1912) can be found again in the *Sonatas Nos. 6, 7 & 8* with the same dynamism, the same violence, the same clear, heavily marked rhythms, in fact with an identical use of simple, short motifs. The *6th, 7th* and *8th Sonatas* were sketched out simultaneously in 1939. Only the 6th had to be finished immediately, the two others being completed in 1942 and 1944. They are generally known as the *War Sonatas*.

The *Sonata No.* 7 won a Stalin prize, as a result of which it gained a particularly resounding reputation, and it is true that it marks a peak in the modern repertoire of piano sonatas. The first movement, which alternates *Allegro inquieto* and *Andantino* opens on persistent marching rhythms. Following on a mood of powerful dynamism and a slight acid piquancy, the atmosphere changes abruptly and a sudden patch of light, in the manner of a reverie, precedes the reprise of the vigorous initial outburst. This play of tension and relaxation is renewed in the second movement, successively *Andante caloroso, Poco piu animato, Piu largamente,*

141

With his second wife Mira Mendelssohn, 1945

Un poco agitato and *Andante caloroso*. This movement, too, is rich in contrasts, with charming phrases supporting a restrained lyricism. The *Finale, Precipitato*, closes the Sonata in an irresistible whirl, a sort of perpetual motion.

Sonatas, operas, ballets, Prokofiev passes easily from one form to the other. Whilst composing the *War Sonatas*, he was brooding on a subject dear to him, a subject which, of all he has dealt with, was to inspire his lyricism and touch the Soviet listener's heart. And so *Cinderella* was born.

Like *Romeo and Juliet, Cinderella* is a ballet lasting a full evening. 'What I wanted to put over essentially in the music of *Cinderella*, he writes, 'was the love of Cinderella and the Prince, the birth and development of this feeling, the obstacles in its way and the realisation of the dream at last. I attached great importance to the "fairy tale" side of it, which posed a series of interesting problems . . .'

We find again in this score the use of the 'leitmotif'. 'Musically speaking, *Cinderella* is characterised by three themes: the first represents her undergoing her ordeals, the second finds her pure and pensive and the third happy and in love. In this way I have tried to project into the music the characters of the charming and dreamy Cinderella, her modest father, her demanding step-mother, her wilful and domineering sisters and the ardent young Prince, so that the audience should not remain indifferent to their difficulties and joys.'

The composer has sought a simplicity and clarity which render the ballet accessible to the widest public. The music is eminently suitable to the requirements of the dance and is in the direct line of the Tchaikovsky ballets. At moments, Prokofiev seems to find it difficult to avoid a certain sentimentality. On the other hand, *The Dancing Lesson* and the *Gallop*, where he gives a free rein to his sense of humour and even to his sense of irony, recall in their vivacity the best passages from *Lieutenant Kizhe* or *The Love of Three Oranges*, the *March* from which is incidentally skilfully quoted in *Cinderella*.

The composition of the ballet *Cinderella* was undertaken in 1940. It was not finished until four years later and the work was performed on 21st November, 1945 on the stage of the Bolshoi Theatre, Moscow. Prokofiev had certainly not taken four years to compose *Cinderella*, but, in the course of his work, the U.S.S.R. had entered the second world war and the Soviet composer could not ignore events of the kind from which the young Russian of 1914 had decided to withdraw.

During the summer of 1941, Prokofiev was at Kratov, with his wife. He had completed a few scenes from *Cinderella* . . .

'On 22nd June, on a warm, sunny morning, I was installed at my work-table. Suddenly, the keeper's wife appeared and asked me anxiously was it true that the Germans were attacking us and bombing our towns. The news staggered me. We went to Eisenstein's place—he was living quite near—and discovered that it was perfectly true. On 22nd June, 1941, the German Fascists attacked Soviet Russia. It was during those days that my plan to compose my opera based on Tolstoi's *War and Peace* took shape. The pages describing the battle of the Russian people against Napoleon in 1812 and the rout of the Napoleonic army suddenly felt very close. It was obvious that just these pages must be the basis of my opera. The destiny of the principal personnages was closely linked with the events of the war.'[1]

And so it was that echoes of the tragic events which were bathing Russia in blood for nearly four years materialised in works of particular resonance. Prokofiev did offer his services in defence of his country, 'but it was his genius that was required of him, not his blood' (Nestiev).

It was into the Opera *War and Peace* that Prokofiev put the best of his genius. The work was spread over about twelve years, and Prokofiev drew up three successive versions. The first consisted of four acts and ten scenes and was performed at the Maly Theatre in Leningrad on 18th April, 1942. Four years later, a second version was completed, considerably amplified, since it had to be performed on two separate evenings. Only the first part was produced in 1946 at the Maly Theatre. A few months before he died, Prokofiev completed the third version, and this

[1] *The Artist and War,* 24th May, 1944 (idem).

was to be the one chosen for the opera's rare performance. In this definitive form, it consists of five acts and ten tableaux.

The adaptation of Tolstoi's enormous novel, made by Mira Mendelssohn-Prokofiev, posed some delicate problems. Numerous episodes had to be sacrificed and the action centred on a few well-characterised personalities. Like the novel, the opera pays equal attention to the psychological and historic aspects of the material and the brief *Overture* suggests this dual atmosphere by the use of heroic fanfares mingled with lyrically tender passages.

The first six tableaux describe the passion of the Prince Andrei Bolkonsky for Natasha, the betrayal of the young girl and the unsuccessful flight with Anatole Kuragin. The ensemble of these six tableaux corresponds to the second book of the novel. The second part of the opera (scenes 7 to 11) recounts the invasion and rout of Napoleon. The seventh scene, widely developed, shows the preparations for the Battle of Borodino (second part of the third book of the novel). Then, like Tolstoi, Prokofiev brings Napoleon on to the scene (scene eight) and Kutusov appears in scenes seven, nine and ten. The ironic, searing scene where Napoleon is surrounded by his Marshals and the Finale to the glory of Kutusov ('Salute to him who has defended our beloved country. Kutusov the brave was our guide in this glorious fight for our liberty and for peace') invites a comparison: in 1942, the two protagonists were Hitler and Stalin. Prokofiev was transposing.

The musical action must, however, take place in 1812 and Prokofiev had recourse during his work of composition to a number of history books and to comments from the poet Davidov. In the Tbilissi library, he found some songs composed among the people during the war of 1812. This latter material he used in the numerous choral parts, the barbarous accents of which often recall *Alexander Nevsky*.

Like *The Love of Three Oranges*, and like *The Flaming Angel*, *War and Peace* is a completely successful achievement. The subject is politico-historic, but Tolstoi's novel inspires the composer more than the edifying verses of Marshak. Musically, Prokofiev avoids both sentimentality and grandiloquence. The lyricism is discreet and the dramatic outbursts are consistently effective. There are no *longueurs* and no dead points; the opera follows a logical progression, with a few peak points here and there: the despair of Natasha (sixth tableau), the great aria of Kutusov in praise of the gilded towers of Moscow (ninth tableau) the frenzy of Andrei (tenth tableau) and the last chorus of soldiers (eleventh tableau). The declamation, too, is in general swift, without any of the chopped style of *The Flaming Angel*. The dramatic quality is nobler and the orchestration, extremely carefully worked out, remains consistently and admirably clear.

Was reality to outdo fiction? The Germans had just declared that the road to Moscow was open and in order to be able to tell the story of the

A still from 'Ivan the Terrible'

Napoleonic defeat in peace, Prokofiev left for Naltchik in August 1941, in company with a group of composers and professors of the Conservatoire of Moscow. Naltchik is a small town situated on the slopes of the Caucasian mountains. Here Prokofiev composed a symphonic suite entitled 1941, inspired by the struggles of the Red Army. The three parts of this suite (*In Battle*; *Night*; *For the Brotherhood of Man*) were the point of departure for the film music of *The Partisans of the Ukrainian Steppes*.

Thanks, so to say, to the war, Naltchik was promoted to the rank of artistic capital of the Soviet Union. The President of the City's Council, conscious of the honour, seized the opportunity to propose to the refugee musicians that they should compile a collection of the folk songs of the province of Kabarda, of which Naltchik is the capital. Why should this original material not create, with the aid of Prokofiev and Miaskovsky, a 'music of Kabarda'? The 23rd Symphony of Miaskovsky and the Quartet No. 2 of Prokofiev may not suffice as a foundation for such music, but they certainly had no other source.

'It seemed to me,' Prokofiev wrote later, 'that the association of original oriental folklore, absolutely new, with the most classic of classical forms such as the string quartet, could yield interesting and unexpected results.'

Knowing well how to avoid facile orientalism and 'local colour' effects, the composer constructed a beautiful quartet which, by the ingenious use of popular themes and a vague hint, at moments, of polytonality, carries a faint Bartokian aroma. It seems clear that Prokofiev, obliged as he was to compose scores based on didactic subjects which inspired him hardly at all, preserves the best of his genius for his chamber music, his sonatas and quartets.

During the course of the autumn of 1941, Prokofiev left Naltchik for Tiflis, where he continued to work with ferocious concentration on *War and Peace*, also finishing the *Piano Sonata No. 7*. But in May 1942, Eisenstein approached him with the suggestion that he should write the music for the film *Ivan the Terrible*, and invited him to join him at Alma-Ata, where the Russian film makers had taken refuge. After a long journey, involving crossing the Caspian Sea, the composer arrived in the capital of Kazakstan, on the borders of Eastern Turkestan.

Eisenstein's plans for *Ivan the Terrible* were that it should be a vast historical canvas in three parts. His plans were, unfortunately, frustrated. The second episode of the film aroused violent controversy in the Soviet Union and the death of Eisenstein prevented the completion of the third part. *Ivan the Terrible* has none of the movement of *Alexander Nevsky*. It is more of a psychological portrait in the Shakespearean manner and a 'series of sumptuous images, admirably composed tableaux and magnificent visions held together by a thread of narrative concerning the deeds and attitudes of the first Tsar of Holy Russia' (Jean Mitry). The music follows the same conception and gains in intensity what it loses in dynamism. The collaboration between musician and producer was so close and the unusual respect of the producer for the music so profound, that certain musical sequences were composed before the scenes were shot and became a point of departure for Eisenstein's direction of them. This procedure, which makes it possible to create a 'whole work of art', is exceptional. Prokofievs are rare and Eisensteins even rarer.

During his stay at Alma-Ata, Prokofiev also composed the *Ballad of the Unknown Boy*, a cantata for operatic tenor, operatic soprano, chorus and orchestra which has not yet been performed outside Russia. 'The subject,' says the composer, 'is the story of the destiny of a boy whose mother and sister have been killed by the Nazis, who have destroyed his childhood happiness. But the child becomes a hero and his courageous act resounds throughout Russia, although his name remains unknown.' This cantata, then, belongs to the strain of Soviet art associated with the terrible war years. It was orchestrated at the end of the summer of 1943, when Prokofiev had installed himself for a few months at Molotov, a little town situated on a tributary of the Volga.

Prokofiev reconciled his creative work in masterly fashion with the enormous amount of travelling he did. As soon as he had finished *Cinderella*, the *Flute Sonata* and the suite from the opera *Simeon Kotko*, he left for Moscow where more manuscript paper awaited him—to be used for the various patriotic *Marches* composed for the First of May (one of which is a *Sketch for a National Anthem*), for the *Piano Sonata No. 8* and, especially, for the *Symphony No. 5*, one of the most famous of Soviet works.

The *Symphony No. 5* is an ambitious work. 'In a way, it crowns a great period of my work,' declared Prokofiev. 'I have thought of it as a work glorifying the human soul . . . In the 5th Symphony I wanted to sing the praises of the free and happy man—his strength, his generosity and the purity of his soul. I cannot say I chose this theme; it was born in me and had to express itself.'

This eloquent manifesto appeared at an opportune moment, for the naive listener might have imagined it was simply a magnificent work of pure music. Whatever the intention, however, the breath of youth with which the *Symphony No. 5* is infused endows it with an undeniable quality of exaltation, so why should Prokofiev not have dedicated it to the 'free and happy man'?

In fact, the *Symphony No. 5* differs profoundly from the four preceding ones. The great constant factors in Prokofiev's work have been many times emphasised in the field of piano, violin, epic and humorous music. It must be admitted that his symphonic work is different in this respect. The first five Symphonies, each with its own particular flavour, could represent different stages in his evolution. The *Classical Symphony* is the elegant play of a young man out to conquer his own métier and win international renown. The *Symphony No. 2* reveals Western influences in the field of harmony. The dramatic quality of the *Symphony No. 3* corresponds to the *Flaming Angel* period, whilst the *Symphony No. 4* matches the bare style of *The Prodigal Son*. Finally, the *Symphony No. 5* is overflowing with humanity, for it is addressed to the huge masses of Soviet people. Moreover, its traditional harmonies permit of its being at the same time accepted by the widest public and clearly placed in the line of Soviet music. But now the evolution has come to an end. The *Symphony No. 6* of 1947 and the final *Symphony No. 7* follow the road pointed out by the 5th.

The *Symphony No. 5*, composed in one month during the summer of

1944, was first performed in Moscow on 13th January, 1945, and in the same year Koussevitsky conducted it before an American public in a performance by the Boston Symphony Orchestra. Its success was immediate and considerable.

After the composition of the *5th Symphony*, the course of Prokofiev's life underwent a change. Just as the war ended and the happy event was saluted by an *Ode to the End of the War*, in which eight harps and four pianos replace string ensembles, Prokofiev's health began to fail. The illness which was to carry him off eight years later now obliged him to cut down on work. He left Moscow and the House of the Soviet Composers' Society of Ivanovo to rest in a quiet country house built on the slopes of the mountain of Nicolino. But Prokofiev never forgot the House of Composers, that veritable musical village, which had enabled him to become better acquainted with the musicians of his country. This house, where he had composed part of the *Sonata No.* 8 and the *Symphony No.* 5 'played a great part in the life of numerous composers during the war years. Created on the foundations of a Sovkhos which was the gift of the Government to the Composers' Society, it was situated,' writes Kabalevsky, 'on the edge of a little stream, dried up in summer. All around, there were fields and, a little further off, enormous forests, the limits of which have so far never been reached. Some composers lived in a large stone house one storey high, which had previously belonged to a rich property owner. Others lived in small cottages surrounding it. The Home was well furnished, cosy and even comfortable. There was a musical instrument in each cottage and the composers who lived in the big house rented work-rooms in the neighbouring village . . .'[1]

Between 1946 and 1950, Prokofiev lived almost constantly in the house at Nicolino with his wife. Later, he simply spent long periods there during the fine weather. The life at Nicolino suited his health and his tastes. He liked long walks, during which he would pick mushrooms (apparently Miaskovsky had taught him this healthy distraction) and enjoyed the simple pleasures of gardening. 'He received his friends,' reports Kabalevsky, 'and showed them round the forest or the garden, of which he was very proud.'[1]

He also, however, kept in touch with Soviet musical life, either by entertaining musicians, whom he questioned tirelessly, or by listening to concert broadcasts. But the limited activity allowed him by his doctors was most of all devoted to the working out of new compositions or the revision of old scores.

Numerous compositions of this last period are still unknown to us, such as the Cantata for the *30th Anniversary of the Revolution*, the opera *The True Man*, the whole of the ballet *The Stone Flower*. On the other hand, scores such as the *Sonata No.* 9, discovered late, or the *Symphony No.* 7, have already conquered a large international audience.

[1]The reminiscences of Kabalevsky (idem).

The case of the *Sonata No. 9*, the last of the series, is especially interesting. In spite of the continuity of Prokofiev's work for piano, this last sounds different. It is marked by an unaccustomed simplicity, clarity and, above all, serenity.

'He told me,' said Madame Mendelssohn-Prokofiev, 'of his desire for a simple, clear, musical language. He had been thinking of it for a long time, persistently, and his thoughts disturbed him profoundly; even when he spoke of clarity and simplicity, he would say that it was not a question of the "old simplicity" which consisted in the repetition of what had already been said, but of a new simplicity, linked with the new direction our lives were taking.'[1]

The *Sonata No. 9*, dedicated to the pianist Sviatoslav Richter, begins with an *Allegretto* where breaths of delicate poetry mingle with touches of humour. This first movement is remarkable for its serene atmosphere and the extreme simplicity of its themes. It is followed by a spare *Allegro strepitoso* and then by an *Andante tranquillo*, a variation in the form of a romance, quiet and rather out of place. But the last bars of the *Andante* announce in the manner of Beethoven the coming of a brisk theme, the motif of the *finale Allegro con brio*. This *finale*, at first only peeping gaily through, at last reveals its true charm and dies away in a gentle reverie.

It is permissible to wonder about the significance of the *Sonata No. 9* completed in 1947 and executed for the first time by Richter on 21st April, 1951. Not only does it end the series of *Sonatas*, but it presents, six years before the death of the composer, his last piano composition, with the exception of the sketches for a 10th and 11th Sonata.

The new tone, more relaxed, quieter, more limpid, can be attributed to the change in character of an ill and ageing man, who has exchanged his youthful energy for a more contemplative attitude to life. But it is perhaps also the successful achievement of the Soviet music to which he was tending, the end of the quest for a 'new simplicity'. The young man once declared: 'To write only according to the rules laid down by previous classics signifies that one is not a master but a pupil'. Later on, the musician perceived that the masses to whom he wanted to address himself could only grasp 'sacred forms' and what had 'already been said'. The task he had assigned himself on his arrival in the Soviet Union was to make himself understood by every kind of public, whilst preserving his personality and taking no refuge in the past. The *Sonata No. 9* seems to establish the perfect achievement of this aim.

Prokofiev, however, passionately, unrestrainedly interested as he was in the new problems presented to Soviet artists, was to become acquainted with the rigours of the Stalin régime after the composition of the *Sonata No. 9*.

[1] The reminiscences of Madame Mendelssohn-Prokofiev (idem).

Prokofiev, Shostakovitch and Khachaturyan

It was a new opera in four Acts, *A True Man*, written in 1947 and 1948, which finally unleashed the 'Prokofiev affair', but the composer was already figuring, in good company, on the 'black list' ten months before the creation of this opera. In fact, on 10th February, 1948, on the occasion of the condemnation of *La Grande Amitié* of V. Muradeli, an Order of the Central Committee of the Communist Party warned musicians against 'a formalist and antipopular direction' and commented: 'This tendency is especially marked in the works of composers such as D. Shostakovitch, S. Prokofiev, A. Khatchaturian, V. Shebalin, G. Popov, N. Miaskovsky, etc. . . . whose work reveals in a particularly obvious way certain formalist deviations and anti-democratic musical tendencies foreign to the Soviet people and their artistic tastes.'

Useless to recall the painful facts connected with the condemnations of 1948. It is enough to illustrate them with an official text and a cartoon:

The official text, signed by Zhdanov, defines the two tasks of the Soviet composer: 'The main thing is to develop and perfect Soviet music. The rest consists in defending Soviet music against the intrusion of decadent bourgeois elements. It should not be forgotten that the U.S.S.R. is now the authentic depository of universal musical culture.'[1]

As for the cartoon, published in *Krokodil* and reported by Pinoteau, this represents a couple stretched out on a bench under a tree in which a bird is singing. The legend runs:

[1]A. Zhdanov. *On Literature, Philosophy and Music.* New Critic Edition 1950.

'Don't you love the way that nightingale is singing?'
'I don't know who wrote the song, so I can't say.'

After the first Decree, the Congress of the Union of Soviet Composers met on 21st December of the same year, less than three weeks after the creation of *The True Man*, in order to inform themselves on the new works performed since the first warning. On the day of the opening of the Congress, the organ of the Propaganda Section of the Central Committee of the C.P. declared:

'The new opera of Prokofiev, produced in Leningrad, shows serious defects from the ideological and artistic point of view. Prokofiev's music is in direct contradiction to the text and dramatic action. The Soviet spectator is outraged to see the pilot, a hero of the war, depicted as a grotesque marionnette. Almost the entire opera is constructed on an unmelodious musical declamation and the few songs introduced by the author cannot save the situation . . .' After the Congress, a letter from Prokofiev was read in which he acknowledged that the criticisms directed against his latest work were justified.

On 13th January, 1949, in *Izvestia*, V. Kukharsky condemned *The True Man* in even more severe terms as 'a striking example of this detachment of the artist from real life, composing his work in the shelter of his ivory tower.'

Finally, Nestiev, Prokofiev's biographer, joined the fray and the perusal of articles by this musicologist is an education. After writing: 'Of the twenty works composed abroad, in particular during the years 1922-1932, almost none, one can say with confidence, will remain in the repertory', he then launched an attack on the work of the Soviet period, accusing the *6th* and *7th Sonatas* and the *6th Symphony* of 'artificial complexity' and proceeding to criticise one after the other of the works one would have imagined out of reach of such attack: the *8th* and *9th Sonatas*, the *5th Symphony* and the *Ode to the End of the War*. To crown this splendid edifice, Nestiev did not hesitate to acknowledge his own errors of judgment: 'The music critic', he declared, 'by approving all the work of these years, was exercising a bad influence on the development of Prokofiev during the period 1942-1947'!

It would be unjust, however, to accuse the Soviet critic of all the misdeeds. Certain Western judgments are also quite rich. In 1951, M. R. Aloys Mooser deplored the fact that the Orchestre Romand, performing Prokofiev's *Symphony No. 6* should 'prostitute its reputation by contact with such insane, base compositions' by a composer who is 'the victim of his own facility and congenital loquacity . . . bereft of the most elementary taste and incapable, apparently, of exerting any control over the quality of the ideas that come into his head . . .'

There is no question of the fiery Prokofiev protesting against the attacks of the Soviet authorities or of taking legal action, as at the time of the *Lifar affair*. He had not even the choice between 'giving in or getting out'. He tried to buy himself back with a popular ballet and a most educative cantata: *Guarding the Peace*. After the attacks to which he had been subjected, one can understand the significance of this statement, frankly recorded by Madame Mendelssohn-Prokofiev: 'I can still see Sergei's anxious expression on waking in the middle of the night before the first performance of the oratorio *Guarding the Peace*, wondering whether he had succeeded in putting into the work what he wanted to express . . .'

Guarding the Peace is an oratorio on a text of the poet Marshak. 'What is the content of this modest work?' asks Prokofiev. '. . . It tells of the difficult days of the Second World War, the tears of mothers and orphans, of towns destroyed by fire and the terrible sufferings of the people . . . In this work I have tried to express my thoughts and ideas on war and peace and the certainty that there will be no more war, that all peoples will fraternise to save civilisation, our children and our future.'

After working with texts from Dostoïevsky, Pushkin, Gozzi, Briussov and Tolstoi, how was it possible for Prokofiev to compose music for such words as Marshak's?

> *A radio communiqué from Washington:*
> '*O.K. Have sent hundreds of thousands of bombs to Europe*'
> *Sealed consignments of bombs in huge cases are hurried to Marseilles*
> *But a French port proudly replies:*
> '*There is no one in our docks to unload the ships*' . . .
> *. . . Everyone must fight for Peace!*
> *Down with the warmongers!*

The music reflects the text, but did not escape Nestiev's thunderbolts. He criticised the 'over-instrumented' prosody and melody (*Soviet Music* 1951). Perhaps, for other reasons than this, it is better to forget a work in which certain reviewers thought they perceived the swan-song of the composer. What would the author of *The Ugly Duckling* have said?

The oratorio was preceded by a ballet: *The Stone Flower*, taken from stories from the Ural by Pavel Bazhov and inspired, according to the author, 'by the joy of creative work addressed to the people, the beauty of the Russian soul, the power and countless wealth of nature, who yields only to the labour of man.'

Finally, as he was composing *Guarding the Peace* and *The Stone Flower* Prokofiev was at the same time once again reserving the best of his inspiration for a chamber music score, a *Sonata for 'Cello and Piano* which enabled him to use for his solo part an instrument which he had employed rather seldom hitherto. It was, in a way, a revelation; he afterwards revised the *'Cello Concerto* which was to become the *Symphonia Concertante Opus* 125, and planned the composition of a *Concertino for 'Cello* and of a *'Cello Sonata*, whose completion was prevented by his death.

The *Sonata for 'Cello and Piano* has not the serenity of the *Sonata No. 9 for Piano*, for the sharply contrasted writing passes abruptly from reverie to passion, but it has a tendency towards lyricism of expression and simplification of idiom. Like the *Symphonia concertante*, it is possessed of a clean-cut harmony which contrasts strongly with the *'Cello Concerto*.

Other compositions of the years 1949-1951 are: *Soldiers' Marching Song*, *Winter Bonfire*, a symphonic suite called *Summer Night* taken from *The Betrothal at the Convent* and several suites from *The Stone Flower* ballet. But the two major works of this period, the last complete scores of the composer, are a 'holiday poem' called *The Meeting of the Volga and the Don Opus* 130 and the *Symphony No. 7 Opus* 131.

Prokofiev himself defined *The Meeting of the Volga and the Don* as follows:

'I am composing a poem for large orchestra', he said in *Les Nouvelles* (1951 No. 10), 'dedicated to the junction of two Russian rivers, the Volga and the Don, so I have called it *The Meeting of the Volga and the Don*. How did this theme occur to me? It was dictated by life. There are numerous popular songs on the two themes and certain more recent ones on the subject of man conquering nature. Can the artist draw apart from life; can he shut himself up in an ivory tower, restrict the scope of his creative work by the play of personal emotions; or should he be present wherever he is needed, where his words and music can help the people to live better and more deeply?'

Again, in *Soviet Art*, he writes, on 17th November, 1951: 'In the course of my work, I have scanned the vastness of our two magnificent rivers, the songs they have inspired in the people and the poems dedicated to them by Russian poets, both classical and contemporary. I am endeavouring to compose music which is easy to sing and which reflects the joy now uplifting our people . . .'

This is the key to the symphonic poem performed for the first time in Moscow on 22nd February, 1952. The score, rich in themes at the same time joyous and solemn, is of a generously lyrical quality; nonetheless, it remains paralysed by density of orchestration and banality of expression.

The same faults spoil a score which, perhaps because it occupies the last place in the chronological catalogue of Prokofiev's work, was repeatedly acclaimed by Western music critics. In fact, according to some reviewers, the *Symphony No. 7* would appear to be the 'musical testament' of the composer, characterised by a drive and lyricism, a return to source which are 'the undeniable signs of a renewed youth'. Such summary judgments omit to point out that youth is usually characterised by excesses, complications, innovations; and that 'testament' simply means a 'deed whereby one declares ones last wishes'. Now, we know that the last wishes of Prokofiev are represented, in fact, by aspirations towards a simplified lyricism, so the explanation, in spite of the magic words 'musical testament', is worthless as an estimate.

The fact is that the *Symphony No. 7*, with its mixed influences of Franck and Tchaikovsky, does not, in spite of fugitive references to *Chout*, succeed in disengaging itself from the composer's prejudiced attitude. The aim achieved in the *Sonata No. 9* is only glimpsed in the *Symphony No. 7*. It is possible that the failure of the work, musically speaking, can also be put down to the failing health of Prokofiev who, from 1950 onwards, had been on the decline. Long periods in hospital had taken their toll more of his creative genius than of his need to create; in fact, Madame Mendelssohn-Prokofiev reports that: '. . . during the last months, all the forces his being could muster were tensed to write down as quickly as possible what he had planned. He worked on seven scores at once. A few days before the end, weakened by a fierce attack of 'flu, Sergei asked me to write the titles of the seven last works in the complete catalogue which we had compiled in 1952. Terrified (for I knew that most of the pieces were mere sketches) I tried to tell him that we had time to do it later, when he had finished the work, but he asked me so repeatedly and so insistently that, not wishing to cross him, I took a notebook and pencil and wrote down to his dictation:

'*Opus 133 : Concerto No. 6 for two pianos and orchestra in three movements.*
Opus 134: 'Cello Sonata in four movements.
Opus 135: Sonata No. 5 for piano in three movements (new edition).
Opus 136: Symphony No. 2 in three movements (new edition).
Opus 137: Sonata No. 10 for piano in E Minor.
Opus 138 : Piano Sonata No. 11.

'Sergei had finished only the second edition of the *Piano Sonata No. 5*. He had done a lot of work on the *Concertino for 'Cello and orchestra* with the collaboration of M. Rostropovitch. The *Concerto No. 6* which Sergei wanted to dedicate to Richter and Vediernikov and the *'Cello Sonata* were mere sketches. He had just begun work on the *Piano Sonata No. 10*. He had written a page and a half of it and had not yet done any work on the *Piano Sonata No. 11*.'

By dictating this catalogue, Sergei Prokofiev showed that he had understood how near he was to the end; he was reaffirming, in the last hour of his life, his powerful urge to create. He died on 7th March, 1953, a few hours after the death of Stalin, of a cerebral haemorrhage, and was buried in Moscow, in the cemetery of the ancient monastery of Novo-Devichy, built by the Duke Vassily IV, father of Ivan the Terrible, not far from the graves of Scriabin and Czechov. *Sovietskoye iskustvo* reported:

'The Soviet composer Prokofiev died, alas, on the day of the tragic announcement of the death of the great Stalin. As a result, it was not possible to announce his death in the Press until a few days later . . .'

Prokofiev Speaks to the Soviet People

M. Larionov 1915 Ugolvy

"Choute"
de Prokofeff

Moscow 1945, a photograph taken by Prokofiev

PROFILE OF PARIS MUSICAL LIFE (1931-1932)

I say 'profile' because I want to pick out the most characteristic traits in our Paris musical life. Of course, I should like to talk to you more than anything about the performance of Soviet compositions but, for once, Paris, this 'junction of all roads' has shown an incomprehensible ignorance and inertia. Apart from my own work, only Mossolov's *Steel Foundry* has captured the attention of musical circles. The immense enthusiasm which Florent Schmitt, a musician known in influential places, has manifested for this work has greatly contributed to its success and to its wide-spread performance. His articles have made possible a second hearing of it in Paris and performances in quite a few towns watchful of the capital's judgment. Its success was of course not unqualified; there were some who tried to show up the 'mechanistic' aspect of the work or its rather forced construction, but the picturesque impression prevailed and the imagination of the Parisians was caught by it.

Among the new attractions in Paris, the new opera by Milhaud, *Maximilian*, inspired high hopes. It was mounted at the Opéra with great care. The historical subject is taken from the life of the one and only Mexican Emperor, Maximilian, who was over-thrown by revolution. This theme seemed to offer opportunities for grandiose crowd scenes, the more so since Milhaud is attracted by large productions with huge choruses. But instead of this he leaned towards the lyrical aspects of the fallen Maximilian's personal emotions. The result, on the stage, was rather long, hence the failure of the opera . . .

... Let us leave musical composition and consider certain peculiaritie of the organisation of Paris musical life: for instance, the quite unusua part played by symphony orchestras. They are numerous in Paris, to numerous even, but their task is conducted without any over-all plan They are all private enterprises, competing and preventing each othe from staying alive. Certain orchestras are established with the help o funds contributed by private persons; others are a sort of independen concern, functioning at their own risk and sharing the benefits ou among the musicians. These have to struggle with the great orchestras organised by private persons, with considerable means available to them Sometimes one independent orchestra becomes the rival of another. O Sundays, for example, about six symphony concerts vie with each othe for an audience at the same hour, and the result is that the halls are neve full. A bad house upsets the budget of an orchestra and prevents it rehearsing sufficiently, to say nothing of the miserable salary which mos musicians have to be content with. And in Paris these musicians are mor often than not of the best quality and can cope with any modern score.

CAN MELODIES RUN OUT?

In a letter addressed to the editor of the journal *The Pioneer* M. Alkine asks:
'Will there come a time in musical development when all melodies and harmonies will run out?'
As so much music has been composed over such a long time, one is obviously tempted to believe that it will soon be impossible to write a new melody without repeating what has already been done.

Let us try to see whether indeed few combinations are possible in composing a melody. Let us take for example the game of chess. I am sure this game is familiar to most readers of *The Pioneer*. I like it very much myself. Well, I knew a chess player once who had the idea he would write a book in which he would give the best solution to any problem. Let us look at the result. The white pieces opening the game have twenty possibilities, with the pawns advancing by one or two squares and the four different moves of the knights. Whatever white does, black has also twenty possibilities. Multiply twenty by twenty and we have already four hundred variants by the second white move or eight thousand by the second black move. By the fourth white move, there will be sixty million and it can still be claimed that the game has not yet begun. So the idea of writing the book had to be abandoned.

What happens in music?

We begin a melody with a certain note; for the second note, we can choose any note in the octave above or below; in the octave above, we have twelve notes, and the same number in the octave below; if one adds to this the original note (for we can repeat the same note in a melody) there will be at our disposal, for the second note in the melody, twenty-five variants, and for the third, twenty-five multiplied by twenty-five, that is six hundred and twenty-five variants. Let us imagine a melody which is not particularly long—say eight notes. How many variants are there for such a melody? Twenty-five multiplied by twenty-five seven times, in other words twenty-five to the seventh power. How many does that make? Take a pencil and paper, fill your sheet up with sums, and you will get nearly six milliard possibilities. There are six milliard combinations from which the composer can choose those which he needs for his melody. But this is not all, for the notes have a different duration and the rhythm completely changes the shape of a melody. Moreover, the harmony and the accompaniment give the melody a totally different character. These six milliard have to be multiplied several times to obtain all the possibilities.

The Pioneer No. 7, 1939.

Opening Prokofiev's Trunk

Scene from the ballet 'Cinderella', staged by L. Lavrovsky

From l. to r. Claude Samuel, FRB and Mario Bois in the cellar of Boosey and Hawkes

OPENING PROKOFIEV'S TRUNK

One morning in summer 1959 I had decided to devote a few hours to something which occupies a large place in the life of an editor: papers and dust. It was no longer the season of evening dress at the Opera, and I took the opportunity to put on a working sweater and go down to the cellars in our music publishing house at 22 rue d'Anjou in Paris. I had recently taken over the management of this house and was curious to explore its entrails.

In 1924, a great gentleman established himself at 22 rue d'Anjou, in Paris: he was Sergei Koussevitsky. He installed his Russian music editions there, which he had brought from Moscow and Leipzig, and assembled other Russian houses there: Gutheil and later Belaieff. The group of The Five were largely outstripped for, along with Cui, Balakireff, Rimsky-Korsakov and Borodin, there were Liadov, Nicolas Tcherepnin, Nabokov, Glazounov, Scriabin and Gretchaninov, old gentlemen mostly, who were to bring new blood to the old body of music in the form of the two young barbarians, Stravinsky and Prokofiev.

Koussevitsky, the Maecenas, the aesthete, the discoverer of genius, received at the rue d'Anjou during the years 1925–1930 the daily visits of the already mature Rachmaninov, of the great Diaghilev, who had not much longer to live, of Rubinstein, of the noisy young Stravinsky, already at the height of his fame, or of the young Prokofiev, who had made a sensation here and there but whose life was still difficult and whose future was still problematic.

163

When I took over this office for the first time, I found in some old drawers a great number of letters signed by Toscanini, Stokowski and Ansermet and in an enormous file marked 'In Heroic Times' a mass of letters of introduction, rough notes, concert programmes with notes such as 'unbearable'; 'divine'; 'very poor'; receipts, draft contracts, restaurant bills—in fact all the small evidences of daily life in which the grandiose and the banal were ludicrously intermingled and all signed Nicolas, Igor or Sergei.

I had not had the opportunity to meet my predecessor. He had a fabulous memory and kept everything in his head; but he had taken his head with him and I found myself in charge of a publishing house where every day brought a new discovery. I knew it would be a delight to bring the past to light here; it was the vague enchantment experienced by children in lofts.

So I went down to the cellar. Two thousand copies of a study for female voice, in Russian; three thousand French libretti of that marvellous legend of the *Invisible Town of Kitej*, the opera by Rimsky-Korsakov; as many of the opera *Mozart and Salieri*, etc. Step by step, layer by layer, case by case we proceeded, making inventories and going through each of the mountains of papers from top to bottom.

Then there emerged from the shadows a trunk: hump-backed, heavy, with massive locks which opened. In the dim light of the electric bulb in the basement, I delved into the dust to find . . . a pair of yellowish pyjamas with brown stripes. On the pocket was embroidered S. P. We brought the lamp up closer. There was a 1938 newspaper cutting: 'Gary Cooper in Paris'. Then a photograph: Sergei Prokofiev with his two sons on his knee.

Then there were stamps 'for the children's collections'; programmes; contracts; a missal curiously accompanied by a number of Christian Science texts (one in Prokofiev's hand, reading: 'I am spiritual, therefore vigorous'); a booklet on similar subjects of which only the title: 'Listening in to an Invisible World' could have concerned the composer; the copied-out words of the French song *Ma Normandie*; the score of a Buxtehude prelude and fugue for organ (transcribed for piano by Prokofiev); a treatise on vowel phonetics; the announcement of a meeting on the 'world's stateless'; a cutting about the revival of *Carmen* at the Opera Comique in the presence of Emma Calve, aged eighty years (celebrated in this role); the programme of performances given by Jean-Louis Barrault of *Numance*, a tragedy by Cervantes (which was to inspire Henry Barraud's opera). And then a card, postmarked Leningrad: 'I am happy about my journey to the U.S.S.R. My three Moscow concerts were all sold out on the same day'. But in the same box there was a child's drawing, with the inscription: 'the train daddy will be coming home on' and the following equally naîve and moving extract from a letter: 'I think of you every day. I am very lonsom (sic) without you. I wish you would come and live with us.'

Obviously, it seemed uncouth to open this trunk in public and reveal all the bits and pieces in it on the pretext that it was Prokofiev who had assembled them. There I was, confronted by my task as publisher. It was a question of moral right, of the total and reciprocal confidence which should bind composer and publisher. Prokofiev had for a long time considered 22 rue d'Anjou as his Paris residence. He had his mail addressed there and left his personal baggage there when he left for the U.S.S.R. in 1938. One obviously has to respect this intimacy, assembly and preserve this precious evidence of the life of a genius, shutting the trunk and affixing a label: 'property of Sergei Prokofiev'.

The adventure came to an end a few days later. Our cellar no longer held any mysteries for me. The Abbé Pierre sent his rag-sorters, who carted away four tons of paper; in their sweeping up operations, I came across them as they were moving the trunk and shouted: 'Hey, no! Not that!'

List of Works

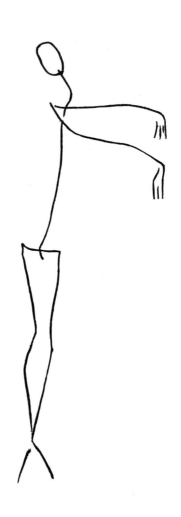

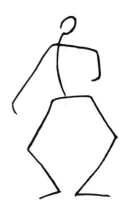

LIST OF WORKS

1907-1909	Op. 1	Piano Sonata No. 1 in F Minor.
1909	Op. 2	Four piano studies.
1911	Op. 3	Four piano pieces: Story; Badinage; March; Phantom.
1910-1912	Op. 4	Four piano pieces: Souvenir; Elan; Désespoir; Suggestion diabolique.
1909-1914	Op. 5	Sinfonietta in A Major.
1910	Op. 6	Dreams: Symphonic tableau for large orchestra.
1909-1910	Op. 7	Two songs for female choir and orchestra based on words by Balmont: The White Swan; The Wave.
1910	Op. 8	Autumnal sketch for small orchestra.
1910-1911	Op. 9	Two romances for voice and piano: Il est d'autres astres (Balmont); The drifting boat (Apoukhtine).
1911	Op. 10	Piano Concerto No. 1 in D Flat Major.
1912	Op. 11	Toccata for Piano in C Major.
1906-1913	Op. 12	Ten piano pieces: Marche; Gavotte; Rigaudon; Mazurka; Caprice; Legende; Prelude; Allemande; Scherzo humoristique; Scherzo.
1912	Op. 12b	Scherzo humoristique added to Op. 12 No. 9.
1911-1913	Op. 13	Magdalen. Opera in one act after the Baroness Lieven.
1912	Op. 14	Piano Sonata No. 2 in D Minor.
1912	Op. 15	Ballade in C Minor for 'Cello and Piano.
1913-1923	Op. 16	Piano Concerto No. 2 in G Minor.
1912-1914	Op. 17	Sarcasms. Five piano pieces.
1914	Op. 18	The Ugly Duckling, after Andersen (for voice and piano; there are two variations for orchestra).
1916-1917	Op. 19	Violin Concerto No. 1 in D Major.
1914	Op. 20	Ala and Lolly. Scythian suite for large orchestra.
1915-1920	Op. 21	Chout (The Buffoon). Ballet in six tableaux. Story by Afanassiev, libretto by Prokofiev.
1922	Op. 21b	Chout. Ballet suite for large orchestra.

1915-1917	Op. 22	Visions fugitives. Twenty piano pieces.
1915	Op. 23	Five poems for voice and piano: Sous le toit (Gorianski); The little grey dress (Hippius); Suis moi sans crainte (Verine); Dans mon jardin (Balmont); The prophet (Agnivtseff).
1915-1927	Op. 24	The Gambler. Opera in four acts and six tableaux after Dostoievsky.
1916-1917	Op. 25	Classical Symphony.
1917-1921	Op. 26	Piano Concerto No. 3 in C Major.
1916	Op. 27	Five poems by Anna Akhmatova for voice and piano: The sun has flooded my room; The true tenderness; Memories of the sun; Bonjour; The King with the grey eyes.
1917	Op. 28	Piano Sonata No. 3 in A Minor from old notebooks.
1917	Op. 29	Piano Sonata No. 4 in C Minor from old notebooks.
1934	Op. 29b	Andante from Sonata No. 4, transcription for symphony orchestra.
1917-1918	Op. 30	They are Seven. Cantata for operatic tenor, mixed chorus and large symphony orchestra after Balmont: Les appels de l'antiquité.
1918	Op. 31	Contes de la Vieille Grand'mère. Four piano pieces.
1918	Op. 32	Four piano pieces: Danze; Minuetto; Gavotte; Valse.
1919	Op. 33	The Love of Three Oranges. Opera in four acts after Gozzi.
	Op. 33b	The Love of Three Oranges. Symphonic suite in six parts.
1919	Op. 33c	The Love of Three Oranges. Two fragments from the Opera transcribed for piano. March and scherzo.
1919	Op. 34	Overture on Jewish themes for clarinet, string quartet and piano.
1934	Op. 34b	Idem for symphony orchestra.
1920	Op. 35	Five songs without words for voice and piano.
1925	Op. 35b	Five songs for violin and piano.
1921	Op. 36	Five poems by Balmont for voice and piano: Incantation, fire and water; Birdsong; The Butterfly; Think of me; The pylons.
1919-1927	Op. 37	The Flaming Angel. Opera in five acts after Brioussov. Libretto by Prokofiev.
1923	Op. 38	Piano Sonata No. 5 in C Major.
1924	Op. 39	Quintet for Oboe, clarinet, violin, viola and double bass in G Minor.
1924	Op. 40	Symphony No. 2 in D Minor.
1925	Op. 41	Le Pas d'Acier (The Steel Trot). Symphonic suite.
1926	Op. 42	American overture in B Major for chamber orchestra; variation for full orchestra (1928).
1925-1929	Op. 43	Divertissement for orchestra.
1928	Op. 43b	Divertissement, transcription for piano.
1928	Op. 44	Symphony No. 3 in C Major.
1928	Op. 45	Things in Themselves, two pieces for piano.
1928	Op. 46	The Prodigal Son. Ballet in three acts. Libretto by B. Kochno.
1929	Op. 46b	The Prodigal Son. Symphonic suite from the ballet.
1930	Op. 47	Symphony No. 4 in C Major.
1929	Op. 48	Sinfonietta for small orchestra in A major.
1931	Op. 49	Four portraits from The Gambler, symphonic suite.
1930	Op. 50	String quartet No. 1.
	Op. 50b	Andante for string quintet from the Quartet.
1930	Op. 51	On the Dnieper. Ballet in two tableaux. Libretto by Sergei Lifar and Prokofiev.
1933	Op. 51b	On the Dnieper. Symphonic suite from the Ballet.
1930-1931	Op. 52	Six piano pieces.
1931	Op. 53	Piano Concerto No. 4 for Left Hand in B Major.
1931-1932	Op. 54	Two Sonatinas for Piano in E Minor and G Major.
1932	Op. 55	Piano Concerto No. 5 in G Minor.
1932	Op. 56	Sonata for two violins in C Major.
1933	Op. 57	Choral Symphony for full orchestra.
1933-1938	Op. 58	'Cello Concerto in E Minor.
1934	Op. 59	Three piano pieces: Promenade; Landscape; Pastoral sonatina.

1934	Op. 60	Lieutenant Kizhe. Symphonic suite from the film music.
1934	Op. 60b	Two songs from the film Lieutenant Kizhe for voice and piano.
1934	Op. 61	Egyptian Nights. Symphonic suite.
1933–1934	Op. 62	Pensées. Three piano pieces.
1935	Op. 63	Concerto No. 2 for violin in G Minor.
1935–1936	Op. 64	Romeo and Juliet. Ballet in four acts and ten tableaux.
1936	Op. 64b	Romeo and Juliet. Symphonic suite No. 1.
1936	Op. 64c	Romeo and Juliet. Symphonic suite No. 2.
1935	Op. 65	Twelve piano pieces for children.
1941	Op. 65b	Summer Day. Children's suite for small orchestra.
1935	Op. 66	(a) Two Choruses (voice and piano): The partisan Gelezniak; Anioutka. (b) Four Choruses: The land awakes; Through snow and fog; Behind the mountain; Voroshilov song.
1936	Op. 67	Peter and the Wolf. Symphonic tale for children with words by Prokofiev.
1936–1939	Op. 68	Three songs for children (voice and piano): Chatterbox (Bartaud); Sweet melody (Sakonsky); The Little pigs (Milkhalkova).
1935–1937	Op. 69	Four military marches.
1936	Op. 70	The Queen of Diamonds, for full symphonic orchestra—film music.
1936	Op. 70b	Boris Godounov. Music for symphony orchestra based on Pushkin's drama.
1936	Op. 71	Eugene Onegin. Stage music.
1936	Op. 72	Russian overture for symphony orchestra. Two variations.
1936	Op. 73	Three romances for voice and piano with words by Pushkin: The fir trees; Crimson dawn; In the prison cell.
1936–1937	Op. 74	Cantata for 20th Anniversary of the October Revolution, for symphony orchestra, military band, accordion band, percussion bands and two choirs, on words from Marx, Lenin and Stalin.
1937	Op. 75	Ten piano pieces from Romeo and Juliet.
1937	Op. 76	Songs of today for solo, choir (mixed) and symphony orchestra: March; Passing over the bridge; Salute; The Golden Ukraine; Brother for Brother; Maidens; The Twenty-year-old; Lullaby; From land to land.
1937–1938	Op. 77	Hamlet. Theatre music for small symphony orchestra.
1938	Op. 77b	Gavotte No. 4 for piano from Hamlet.
1938–1939	Op. 78	Alexander Nevsky. Cantata for mezzo-soprano, choir and orchestra.
1939	Op. 78b	Alexander Nevsky. Three songs from the film.
1939	Op. 79	Seven songs for voice and piano: Fatherland song; Stachanovka; On the Polar seas; Adieux; Courage; Forward!; Cossack March; To the Road!
1938–1946	Op. 80	Sonata No. 1 for violin and piano in F Minor.
1939	Op. 81	Simeon Kotko. Opera in five acts and seven tableaux from the Kataev narrative: I am the son of the working people. Libretto by Kataev and Prokofiev.
1941	Op. 81b	Symphonic suite for full orchestra from Simeon Kotko.
1939–1940	Op. 82	Piano Sonata No. 6 in A Major.
1939–1942	Op. 83	Piano Sonata No. 7 in B flat Major.
1939–1944	Op. 84	Piano Sonata No. 8 in B flat Major.
1939	Op. 85	Hymn to Stalin. Popular texts for mixed choir and orchestra.
1940	Op. 86	Betrothal in a Monastery. Opera in four acts and nine tableaux. Libretto by Prokofiev, based on Sheridan's Duenna.
1940–1944	Op. 87	Cinderella. Ballet in three acts. Libretto by Volkov.
1941	Op. 88	Symphonic March for full orchestra in B Major.
1941–1942	Op. 89	Seven songs for choir, solo voice and piano and a March in A Flat Major: Admiral Trash (Mayakovsky); Song of the Brave (M. Mendelssohn); The Tankman's vow (M. Mendelssohn); Son of Kabardi (M. Mendelssohn); The Soldier's Sweetheart (M. Mendelssohn);

		Fritz (M. Mendelssohn); A Soldier's Love (M. Mendelssohn).
1941	Op. 90	1941. Symphonic suite for full orchestra in three parts: Night; During the Battle; For the Brotherhood of man.
1941–1952	Op. 91	War and Peace. Opera in five acts and ten tableaux after Tolstoy. Libretto by M. Mendelssohn and Prokofiev.
1941	Op. 92	String Quartet No. 2 in F Major on Kabaldina Balkan themes.
1942–1943	Op. 93	Ballad of an Unknown Child. Cantata for soprano, tenor, chorus and orchestra. Libretto by Antokolski.
1943	Op. 94	Sonata for flute and piano in D Major.
1944	Op. 94b	Sonata No. 2 for violin and piano in D Major, transcription from the above.
1942	Op. 95	Three piano pieces from Cinderella: Intermezzo; Gavotte; Slow Waltz.
1941–1942	Op. 96	Three piano pieces: Waltz from War and Peace; Contredanse; Waltz.
1943	Op. 97	Ten piano pieces from Cinderella.
1944	Op. 97b	Adagio for violin and piano from Cinderella.
1943	Op. 98	Sketches for a National Anthem.
1943–1944	Op. 99	March for orchestra; in B Major.
1944	Op. 100	Symphony No. 5 in B flat Major.
1946	Op. 101	Romeo and Juliet. Suite No. 3 for orchestra from the ballet.
1944	Op. 102	Six piano pieces from the ballet Cinderella.
1947	Op. 103	Piano Sonata No. 9 in C Major.
1944	Op. 104	Vocal and piano arrangements of popular Russian songs.
1945	Op. 105	Ode to the End of the War, for eight harps, four pianos and orchestra of wind instruments, percussion and double bass.
1945	Op. 106	Two Duets, arrangements for tenor, bass and piano of Russian popular songs.
1946	Op. 107	Cinderella. Symphonic suite No. 1 from the ballet.
1946	Op. 108	Cinderella. Symphonic suite No. 2 from the ballet.
1946	Op. 109	Cinderella. Symphonic suite No. 3 from the ballet.
1946	Op. 110	Waltz suite for symphony orchestra: Since I have known you (War and Peace); Cinderella in the castle (Cinderella); Mephisto Waltz (Lermontov); The end of the story (Cinderella); The Waltz of the New Year Ball (War and Peace); Meeting with happiness (Cinderella).
1945–1947	Op. 111	Symphony No. 6.
1947	Op. 112	Symphony No. 4 in C Major (revised).
1947	Op. 113	Festive overture for symphony orchestra.
1947	Op. 114	Flourish, all-powerful land. Cantata for 30th anniversary of the Revolution, for mixed choir and orchestra, based on texts by Dolmatovsky.
1947	Op. 115	Sonata for solo violin in D Major.
1942–1945	Op. 116	Ivan the Terrible. Film music.
1947–1948	Op. 117	A True Man. Opera in four acts after Polevoy. Libretto by M. Mendelssohn-Prokofiev and the author.
1948–1950	Op. 118	The Stone Flower. Ballet in four acts based on the story by Bazhov. Libretto by Lavrovsky and M. Mendelssohn-Prokofiev.
1949	Op. 119	Sonata for violin and piano in C Major.
1949	Op. 120	Waltzes for symphony orchestra from Pushkin.
1950	Op. 121	Soldiers' Marching Song. Words by Lugovsky.
1949	Op. 122	Winter Woodpile. Children's suite for choir and orchestra. Words by Marshak.
1950	Op. 123	Summer Night. Symphonic suite from Betrothal in a Convent.
1950	Op. 124	Guarding the Peace. Oratorio for mezzo-soprano, mixed choir, children's choir and orchestra. Words by Marshak.
1950–1952	Op. 125	Sinfonia concertante for 'Cello in E Minor.

1951	Op. 126	Wedding suite from the ballet The Stone Flower for full orchestra.
1951	Op. 127	Gipsy Fantasy for full orchestra from the ballet The Stone Flower.
	Op. 128	Rhapsody on the Urals for full orchestra from the ballet The Stone Flower.
	Op. 129	The Lord of the Copper Mountain. Symphonic suite from the ballet The Stone Flower.
1951	Op. 130	Celebration poem: The Meeting of the Volga and the Don.
1951-1952	Op. 131	Symphony No. 7 in C sharp Minor.
1952	Op. 132	Concertino for 'Cello and orchestra in G Minor.
1952	Op. 133	Concerto No. 6 for two pianos and string orchestra.
	Op. 134	Sonata for solo 'Cello.
1952-1953	Op. 135	Piano sonata No. 5, revised.
	Op. 136	Symphony No. 2, revised.
1953	Op. 137	Sonata No. 10 for piano. Only the first forty-four bars completed.
	Op. 138	Sonata No. 11 for piano.

No opus number: Five popular songs from Kazakstan.
Music for the film Kotovsky.
Music for the film Tonia.
Music for the film Partisans in the Ukrainian steppes.
Schubert/Prokofiev: Selected waltzes collected into a suite.
(a) for piano with two hands.
(b) for piano with four hands.

Chronology

CHRONOLOGY

	PROKOFIEV	COMPOSITIONS
1891	Birth of Sergei Prokofiev at Sonsovka.	
1892		
1893		
1895		
1896		
1897		
1899	Journey to Moscow. Revelation of Opera.	
1901		
1902	First lessons with Gliere.	
1904	Enters St. Petersburg Conservatoire.	
1905		
1907		*Piano Sonata No. 1.*
1908	Execution of a *Symphony* with no opus number 31.12: First public recital by composer of Op. 3 and 4.	
1909		*Sinfonietta in A Minor.*

THE OTHERS

Birth of Honegger.
Birth of Milhaud.
Death of Tchaikovsky.
Birth of Hindemith.
Death of Brückner.
Death of Brahms.
Tolstoi's *Resurrection*.

Death of Verdi.
Debussy: *Pelléas & Mélisande*.
Death of Dvořák.
Birth of Dallapiccola.
Birth of Kabalevsky.
Russo-Japanese war.
Chekhov: *The Cherry Orchard*.
Birth of Shostakovitch.
Death of Grieg.
Rimsky-Korsakov: *Le Coq d'Or*.
Death of Rimsky Korsakov.
Birth of Messiaen.

Death of Albeniz.
First Diaghilev season.
Death of Balakirev.

1910	6.3: First recital of *Sonata No. 1*.	
1911		*Piano Concerto No. 1.*
1912	7.8: First Moscow performance of *Concerto No. 1*.	*Toccata Op. 11.* *Sonata No. 2 for Piano.*
1913	5.9: First Moscow performance of *Concerto No. 2*.	*Piano Concerto No. 2.*
1914	Rubinstein Prize. Attends performances of Ballets Russes in London.	*The Ugly Duckling.* *Scythian Suite.*
1915		
1916	21.1: First performance of *Scythian Suite* at St. Petersburg.	
1917	Summer: Prokofiev joins his mother at Kislovodsk.	*Violin Concerto No. 1* (begun 1916); Twenty *Visions fugitives* (begun 1915); *Classical Symphony* (begun 1916).
1918	March: Moscow 27.5: Departure for U.S.A. 20.11: First recital in U.S.A.	*They are Seven* (begun 1917).
1919		*The Love of Three Oranges.*
1920		*Chout* (begun 1915).
1921	7.5: 1st performance of *Chout* in Paris. Summer: visit to Britain. 30.12: first performance of *The Love of Three Oranges* in Chicago.	*Piano Concerto No. 3* (begun 1917).
1922	March: installed at Ettal.	
1923	October: settles in Paris.	
1924		
1925	Tours in Berlin and U.S.A.	*The Steel Trot.*
1926	Italian tours.	
1927	Triumphant tours in U.S.S.R.	*The Gambler* (begun 1915). *The Flaming Angel* (begun 1919).
1928	14.6: Koussevitsky directs 2nd Act of *The Flaming Angel* in Paris.	*Symphony No. 3.* *The Prodigal Son.*
1929		
1930	Tour of U.S.A., Cuba and Canada.	
1932	Tour of U.S.S.R. Takes part in foundation of 'Triton' in Paris.	
1933	Return to the Soviet Union.	
1934		*Lieutenant Kizhe.*
1935		*Violin Concerto No. 2.*

Death of Tolstoi.
Death of Mahler.
Ravel: *Daphnis and Chloé*.
Schoenberg: *Pierrot Lunaire*.

Birth of Britten.
29.5: First performance of
Stravinsky's *Sacre du Printemps*.

Outbreak of First World War.
First Charlie Chaplin film.

Death of Scriabin.
Einstein's second theory of
relativity.

Lenin: *Imperialism: Supreme
Platform of Capitalism*.

Russian Revolution. Lenin
comes to power.

Armistice.
Death of Debussy.
Death of Cui.

Death of Saint-Saëns.

Stalin, General Secretary
Communist Party.
Mussolini in power.

Schoenberg: *Five Piano
pieces* Op. 23.

Death of Fauré.
First performance in Berlin
of *Wozzeck* by Berg.

Economic crisis.
Condemnation of literary
formalism in Russia.
Death of Diaghilev in Venice.

Birth of the Third Reich.

Death of Berg.
Death of Dukas.

1936		*Romeo and Juliet* (begun 1935). *Peter and the Wolf*.
1937		
1938	Last of Prokofiev's Western tours.	
1939		*Alexander Nevsky*.
1940	23.6: First performance of *Simeon Kotko* in Moscow.	
1941	Summer: Kratov, then Naltchik. Autumn: Tiflis.	*War and Peace* (repeated 1952).
1942	May: rejoins Eisenstein at Alma-Ata.	*Piano Sonata No. 7* (begun 1939).
1944	Ivanovo.	*Cinderella* (begun 1940). *Symphony No. 5*.
1945		*Ivan the Terrible* (begun 1942).
1946	Nicolino.	
1947		*Piano Sonata No. 9*.
1948	10.2: Warned by C.P. Central Committee. 21.12: Violent attacks from Congress of Soviet Composers' Union against *A True Man*.	
1950	Prokofiev's health on the decline. 19.12: First performance of *Guardians of the Peace* (Moscow).	*Guardians of the Peace*.
1951		*Symphony No. 7*.
1953	7.3: Death of Sergei Prokofiev. 25.11: First concert performance of *The Flaming Angel* (Paris).	

Death of Glazounov.
Bartok: *Music for strings,
percussion and celeste*.
Spanish revolution.
Death of Ravel.
Death of Roussel.

Second World War.
Russo-German pact.

Hitler invades Russia.

Germans held before Stalingrad.

End of Second World War.
Atomic bombs on Hiroshima and
Nagasaki.
Webern assassinated.
Death of Falla.

Death of Schoenberg.
7.3: Death of Stalin.

Iconography

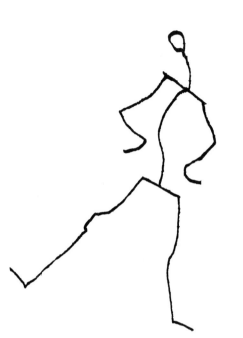

ICONOGRAPHY

We would particularly like to thank Michael Larinov for his important contribution in so kindly making his collection available (see pp. 7, 10, 18, 30, 44, 49, 70, 88, 116, 128, 156, 168, 169, 177, 184, 188). We would also like to thank Editions Boosey and Hawkes of Paris who lent the documents reproduced on pp. 62, 79, 113, 122, 123, 157. Bibliothèque Nationale: pp. 15, 20, 23, 26, 28, 32, 37, 38, 47, 50, 75, 76, 94, 108, 110, 120, 134, 142. Bibliothèque de l'Opéra: pp. 48, 53, 84, 98, 99, 118. Fred Brommet: p. 78. Cinémathèque français: pp. 65, 145. Femina: p. 95. Institut Byzantin: p. 14. Klein: p. 130. Collection Lifar: p. 107. Lipnitzky: p.92. Librairie du Globe: p. 138. Mermod: p. 83. Regards: p. 67. Theodore Stravinsky: p. 51. Roger Viollet: pp. 72, 100. Soviet Bureau of Information: p. 150. Roche: pp. 62, 163. Archives Seuil: p. 161. The sketch by Jacoulov reproduced on p. 98 is taken from *L'Art du Ballet,* by Boris Kochno, published by Hachette. Illustrations on pp. 2, 66, 68, 114, 125, 126, 162 are taken from *S. Prokofiev. Autobiography. Articles. Reminiscences.* published by Foreign Languages Publishing House, Moscow.

Index

In the same series

Bruckner
by Hans-Hubert Schönzeler

Handel
by Stanley Sadie

Liszt
by Claude Rostand

Mozart
by Stanley Sadie

Stravinsky
by Robert Siohan

Tchaikovsky
by Michel Hoffman

Verdi
by Pierre Petit

Wagner Opera
by Audrey Williamson

192